RAILROADS

of the

EASTERN SHORE

LORETT TREESE

THE History PRESS

Published by The History Press
Charleston, SC
www.historypress.com

Front cover, above: Steamboat at Railway Depot, Cape Charles, circa 1950. *Kirk C. Mariner Collection, Eastern Shore Public.*
Front cover, below: Morning Train entering Cape Charles, circa 1920. *Cape Charles Historical Society, Photograph Collection.*
Back cover, below: NYP&N Locomotive No. 30, circa 1900. *Cape Charles Historical Society, Photograph Collection.*

First published 2021

Manufactured in the United States

ISBN 9781467147026

Library of Congress Control Number: 2020948659

For Matthew A. Treese

Contents

Acknowledgements

This book could not have been written without the assistance of many people who work as archivists, librarians and curators of image and manuscript collections.

Special thanks to the librarians at Hagley Museum and Library and in particular to the dedicated staff members who oversee the Manuscripts and Archives Department in Hagley's repurposed "Soda House." They introduced me to the indices and voluminous materials relating to the Pennsylvania Railroad and its subsidiaries.

I would like to thank the staff of the Cape Charles Historical Society at the Cape Charles Museum and Welcome Center. Executive Director Kimberly Leake Denny devoted considerable time helping me with the society's extensive photograph collection documenting the early history of the New York, Philadelphia and Norfolk Railroad in Cape Charles City. Thanks also to Marion Naar and Bill Neville, officers of the society, and local photographer and railroad historian Ed Sharpe, who recently donated his photograph collection to the society.

In addition, I'd like to thank Susan K. Anderson, the archivist at the library and archives of the Philadelphia Museum of Art, who guided me through the Cassatt family correspondence housed in the Perelman Building. Stacia Childers, local history and public services librarian at the Eastern Shore Public Library, helped greatly with images on the website the Countryside Transformed, created by the Eastern Shore Public Library and the Virginia Center for Digital History of the University of Virginia.

I would also like to extend my thanks to the library staff at the Historical Society of Pennsylvania in Philadelphia and the Railroad Museum of Pennsylvania in Ronks, the manuscripts and photo archivists at the Chester County Historical Society in West Chester, the Queen Anne's Railroad Society and my former colleagues at the Bryn Mawr College Library, especially those who handle image requests and expedite interlibrary loans.

My husband and I would like to thank the many guides and docents who contributed their time and personal insight while guiding us through the historical sites of the Eastern Shore, including the Eastern Shore Railway Museum in Parksley, Virginia; Ker Place at the Historical Society of the Eastern Shore of Virginia in Onancock, Virginia; and Mount Harmon Plantation in Earleville, Maryland.

Finally, I would like to thank my husband, Matthew A. Treese, who accompanied me on all my railroad heritage explorations on the Eastern Shore. His experience as a corporate controller was very valuable for my understanding of how American business works.

Introduction

Early in September 1881, George Roberts, president of the Pennsylvania Railroad Company (PRR, or Pennsy), received a letter from Milton Courtright, a well-known railroad contractor and civil engineer. Mr. Courtright got right to the point, opening with the sentence, "I think you will make a mistake if you let the extension of your East Shore line to Cherry Stone go out of your control." Citing the many potential financial rewards to the Pennsy of efficient transportation between Philadelphia and Norfolk via the underserved Delmarva Peninsula, he concluded, "I cannot but think your company ought to avail itself of its advantages at once," before someone else does, he implied.

The concept of a railroad running down the eastern shore of the Chesapeake Bay, forming a link in a land-water transportation route between Philadelphia and Norfolk, and therefore America's North and South, was nothing new in the 1880s. The State of Maryland had granted a charter to a company proposing a railroad from Elkton, Maryland, to Tangier Sound in 1833, when railroading was very young, but its tracks were never built. The idea was revisited by Virginia in the 1850s, when the commonwealth issued charters for two railroads running down Virginia's eastern shore, but neither of these was constructed either. The Delaware Railroad, chartered in 1836 and constructed during the 1850s, ran most of the length of tiny Delaware. It had a Chesapeake port of sorts in Seaford, far up the Nanticoke River, but its main line terminated abruptly at Delmar, a railroad town on the border between Delaware and Maryland. In 1859, work began on Maryland's

Eastern Shore Railroad, intended to link Delmar with Tangier Sound, where steamboats would complete the route to Norfolk, but little construction was completed on this project before the Civil War put an end to commerce and passenger travel between the North and South.

Why would Milton Courtright think that the mighty Pennsylvania Railroad should take on this long-intended short line? Ever since it was chartered in 1846, the Pennsylvania Railroad's directors had aggressively expanded their railroad's reach, mainly by acquiring other railroads, a program they accelerated when the Civil War was over. The Pennsy leased railroads, giving it access to Chicago, Cincinnati and St. Louis, and backed a subsidiary that took its trains into Washington, D.C. Earlier in 1881, the Pennsy had gotten control of the Philadelphia, Wilmington and Baltimore Railroad (PWB), which had been profitably running trains between Philadelphia and Baltimore since the 1830s. Because the PWB controlled the Delaware Railroad, whose construction it had financed, the Pennsy's sudden and surprising acquisition of the PWB meant that it then had half a route between Philadelphia and Norfolk already constructed and operating.

PRR president George Roberts would have known that the difficulty in extending the Pennsy's reach down the rest of the Delmarva Peninsula would not be laying the new tracks over relatively flat geography or operating steamships to take freight and passengers across the Chesapeake Bay, whose waters rarely froze. The project would require authorization from two states and cooperation from various local authorities and community leaders, not to mention a receptive state of mind from the southerners, who would be doing business with Yankees. And President Roberts also would have known that in the 1870s, when Pennsy executives tried to use a holding company called the Southern Railway Security Company to acquire independent southern railroads that could potentially be merged into a network, the project failed due to one of the nineteenth century's notable financial panics, as well as southern suspicion that this was just some carpetbagging swindle.

Although there are no documents to prove that it actually happened, several historians have referred to a meeting held sometime in 1880, when PRR president George Roberts was formally approached about building a railroad connecting Delmar with a new port at the southern end of the Delmarva Peninsula, where specialized vessels would depart for Norfolk. Most historians credit the idea to William L. Scott, a wealthy businessman and coal magnate from Erie who had provided assistance to the Pennsy in the past. Alexander J. Cassatt, then a PRR vice president, claimed that the idea had been his in an article later published in a business publication.

The authors of a comprehensive authorized PRR history published in 1949 credit the idea to Thomas A. Scott (no relation to William), who had been PRR president from 1874 to 1880 and a great advocate of PRR expansion in the South. In any case, despite the urgings of influential contemporaries like Milton Courtright, Roberts purportedly declined the opportunity, leaving William L. Scott and Alexander J. Cassatt to pursue the dream on their own—or so the story goes.

In the meantime, two Pennsylvania businessmen who happened to be brothers, William and Uriah Hunt Painter, had been planning to build and operate much the same railroad through Delmarva ever since the mid-1870s but had been stalled by financial difficulties and insufficient capital. Just a few days before Milton Courtright's letter landed on George Roberts's desk, Roberts's assistant had sent one of the Painter brothers a handwritten draft for a traffic agreement between the Painters' yet unbuilt Peninsula Railroad Company; the Philadelphia, Wilmington and Baltimore Railroad; their lessee the Delaware Railroad; and the Pennsy. The same assistant sent the same document to William L. Scott for his review on November 19 at the request of PRR vice president Alexander J. Cassatt.

The timing seems to indicate that the Pennsy had found a way to do precisely what Mr. Courtright had proposed but in a way that would not repeat the public relations disaster of their Southern Railway Security Company. The long-anticipated line reaching into the South would ostensibly be an independent railroad named the New York, Philadelphia and Norfolk Railroad Company (NYP&N), but the Pennsy would keep operations well under PRR control. The final version of the traffic agreement was signed in May 1882 by George Roberts, William Painter and Alexander J. Cassatt.

Cassatt became NYP&N president in 1885, though he might have been unofficially involved in supervising the construction of its route and its terminal at Cape Charles City, Virginia, following his suspiciously early resignation from the PRR in 1882. He remained involved in the management of the NYP&N until his death in 1906, despite his elevation to PRR president in 1899. Contemporary journalists sometimes called the NYP&N the Cassatt Road.

The Pennsy took direct control of the NYP&N after Cassatt's death by purchasing the majority of its stock. But the executives at the Pennsy had always dominated its board of directors, together with members of the Painter, Scott and Cassatt families. Perhaps Cassatt's resignation from the Pennsy at the age of forty-two had merely freed him to act more or less covertly in the interests of the railroad where his loyalty remained.

No matter who was really in charge, the new line to Norfolk was a well-run operation that did indeed link the postwar North and South, making a trip from Philadelphia to Norfolk shorter and faster than a trip from Philadelphia to Pittsburgh. The New York, Philadelphia and Norfolk Railroad also dramatically transformed the eastern shore of the Chesapeake from a backward backwater into some of the most profitable agricultural real estate in America and a popular destination for vacationers, boat owners and sportsmen, which it has remained. You won't see many trains in operation if you drive the length of the Delmarva Peninsula today, but the Pennsy and the NYP&N played critical roles in the history of the Eastern Shore.

1

Before There Were Railroads

In the decades following the Civil War, the Gilded Age swells dining in the finer restaurants of America and Europe knew little about the eastern shore of the Chesapeake Bay, except that it was the place from which some of their favorite delicacies came. Canvasback ducks thrived there with other choice game birds like woodcocks and partridges. So did diamond-backed terrapin, which were sometimes cooked "Maryland-style" by Baltimore caterers before being shipped out in quart and gallon containers.

Following the Civil War, crabmeat became fashionable, and the Chesapeake Bay became the place to obtain it, once the waters around New York became fished out (or rather crabbed out). Gourmets came to appreciate the creatures known as soft shell crabs, meaning crabs captured after they had molted their shells and before they could grow new ones. During this time, they hid in the grass or sand of the bay's shallows, and Chesapeake children contributed to their families' finances by wading in shallow water and kicking them loose with their bare feet.

Chesapeake oysters had been popular since the early nineteenth century, and by its closing years, they were shipped to all major East Coast cities, and even to Europe, alive in their shells. They were packed in barrels mouth up and refreshed every day or two of their ocean voyage with sea water. When they were served to European royalty, sometimes their shells would be sandpapered smooth and clean for a more elegant presentation. The less exalted could purchase Chesapeake oysters shucked and packed in cans.

Less exotic but equally tasty were the corn, tomatoes, peas, beans, white and sweet potatoes, peaches and berries harvested on Delmarva Peninsula farms. The Gulf Stream made the area a garden, ameliorating a humid climate with ocean breezes that gave it a mean temperature between seventy-four and seventy-seven degrees in the summer and a mild thirty-four to thirty-eight degrees in the winter. Some late-nineteenth-century writers compared the climate to that of Italy.

But the same writers had to acknowledge that the place was more than a little backward. In an 1879 article published by *Harper's New Monthly Magazine*, Howard Pyle described how American culture seemed to have spread rapidly westward to places like Texas, California, Colorado and even Alaska, while the Chesapeake Bay's eastern shore had become a bypassed backwater, seemingly cut off from modern America. His own exploration had shown him that the Eastern Shore got more and more backwatery the farther south one went. Pyle wrote, "In short, the Virginia portion of the peninsula seems sunk in a Rip Van Winkle sleep that has lasted a hundred instead of twenty years, and that as yet shows but small signs of awakening."

The island community of Chincoteague, Virginia, had a rustic tourist attraction, which Pyle had covered in an article for *Scribner's Monthly* two years earlier. Wild ponies had roamed free on neighboring Assateague Island since their ancestors survived shipwreck before White settlers made this area home. These shaggy creatures were periodically rounded up and swum across a channel to Chincoteague, where they were penned up to be branded and sold. Visitors arrived to watch the spectacle via what Pyle described as a "wheezing little steamboat" named *Alice*. Pyle noted that Chincoteague had the potential of attracting sportsmen and those who enjoyed sea bathing—if only the potential tourists had an easy way to get there.

Also limiting Chincoteague's tourism industry was the lack of amenities. Pyle wrote, "The chief restaurant of Chincoteague is a piece of sail elegantly draped over a few upright posts, with a canvas streamer above it bearing conspicuously the sign, 'Stewed Oysters.'" If you wanted to board with a Chincoteague family, "You pick your way with some trouble through a flock of geese, over a pig, a dog, and probably a nearly naked baby rolling over the floor, and find yourself at last safely ensconced in a rickety chair."

As you traveled back north through southern and central Delaware, things got better. There were farms boasting modern improvements giving way to mills and factories that lent the area the pace and prosperity of a place like Connecticut. What made the difference? These Delaware communities were served by modern railroads, while those of the lower Eastern Shore were not.

Although Pyle had his fun with sardonic descriptions of the Eastern Shore lifestyles of hicks and farmers, he never complained about the food. He ended his 1879 article with the observation, "No matter how poor these people are, they always manage to live well, having for their every meal what people of the outside world consider dainties."

The several Europeans who could claim to have discovered the Chesapeake Bay and its eastern shore were not looking for something to eat but rather a shortcut to the Pacific Ocean and the wealth of the Far East. Just five years after Columbus arrived in the Western Hemisphere, Henry VII of England commissioned John Cabot to sail west on a voyage of discovery. Cabot departed from Bristol, sailed around Ireland and then due west, hoping to land somewhere in Japan. He was actually following an old Norse route, which took him to North America. He sailed south along its coast and certainly passed the Chesapeake Bay, which he might or might not have entered. Cabot might have explored the American coast as far south as Florida, but no proof has yet surfaced indicating Cabot ever returned from that voyage.

In 1523, Francis I of France commissioned Giovanni da Verrazzano to find a western route to Asia through North America, which was by that time recognized as a separate continent, but hopefully a narrow one that was penetrated by a water route. Like Cabot, Verrazzanno sailed along the American coast looking for a place where the land would end. He likely missed the mouths of the Chesapeake and Delaware Bays and is today remembered mainly for having mistaken Pamlico Sound west of the Outer Banks for the Pacific Ocean.

Verrazzanno and some of his crew went ashore to explore the forests emitting a sweet smell strong enough to be noticed offshore. He named the place Arcadia, but today, we have no idea exactly where he landed. Claims have been made for North Carolina's Outer Banks or the Atlantic side of the Eastern Shore in what is now Worcester County, Maryland, or Accomack County, Virginia.

Spain had already claimed North America, which it named La Florida. In 1521, Luis Vazquez de Ayllon, a judge in Santo Domingo, commanded Francisco Gordillo and Pedro de Quejo to reconnoiter the North American coast for a shortcut to the Pacific. Instead, they found a land with a pleasant climate, which they named Chicora. Quejo returned in 1525 and discovered the mouth of the Chesapeake. The date was July 2, the feast of St. Mary, so Quejo named the body of water the Bahia de Santa Maria, by which name it subsequently appeared on Spanish maps.

In 1526, the Spaniards tried to found a North American colony in Chicora. Hundreds of men, women, children, priests and slaves landed that fall and established a settlement they named San Miguel de Guadalupe. The effort was abandoned a few months later, following a devastating epidemic. The settlement's location remains unknown, but claims have been made for Wilmington, North Carolina; Winyah Bay, South Carolina; Sapelo Sound, Georgia; and even the site of the future Jamestown.

The Spaniards made a second attempt in 1570, somewhere on the western shore of the Chesapeake, but the settlers were massacred by Native Americans. Spain then gave up on colonizing North America.

England had pretty much stayed out of the New World for reasons related to the melodramatic matrimonial aspirations, not to mention the actual marital history, of Britain's Tudor rulers. But the dynamics of the relationship between sixteenth-century England and Spain changed dramatically with England's defeat of the Spanish Armada in 1588. Following an extended naval war, British king James I made peace with Spain in 1604, paving the way for the English to stake a real claim in the New World.

In 1606, King James I granted a charter to the Virginia Company, which had been formed by ambitious merchants, soldiers and country gentlemen. In 1607, three British ships under the command of Captain Christopher Newport entered the Virginia capes. The passengers landed and began building a fort at a place they named Jamestown. These first colonists were directed to live off the land, survey and map the bay and its tributaries to see if they could discover a shortcut to the Pacific Ocean and incidentally look around for survivors from the lost colony of Roanoke, in case any of them had made their way to the shores of the Chesapeake. In 1609, the first women arrived in Jamestown, followed by the rest of Jamestown's English settlers in 1610.

The Chesapeake where they settled had been formed by a meteor crater some thirty-five million years earlier. When the Ice Age ended, water ran down from nearby mountains and mixed with sea water, filling the crater and creating broad rivers feeding a large estuary punctured by peninsulas. Sea grasses grew in the mixture of fresh water and salt. The bay became an environment where fish and shellfish thrived and, perhaps more important to Europeans in the seventeenth century, a place where ocean-going vessels could find sheltered anchorages. The land surrounding the bay was forested, fertile and nearly flat—very appealing to Englishmen who shared the belief that land was meant to be "improved" and its natural resources developed for profit.

The Virginia colony's objectives sent Captain John Smith (of Pocahontas fame) on two expeditions to the Eastern Shore in 1608, where he became the first recorded European to set foot. Smith's first expedition took him from Cape Henry across the bay, where he encountered a grouping of islands that he named for himself: Smith's Isles. On the Eastern Shore mainland at Cape Charles, he first met up with two "grimme and stout" Native Americans who were spear fishing. Smith wrote, "They boldly demanded what we were, and what we would; but after many circumstances, they in time seemed very kinde," and they directed Smith north to a place called "Acawmacke… where we were kindly treated" by other Native Americans. The reaction was somewhat less welcoming among Native Americans along a river Smith recorded as the Wighcocomoco: "The people at first with great furie seemed to assault us; yet at last with songs, daunces, and much mirth."

Geographically, the Eastern Shore seemed less than hospitable to Smith. He found it to be a place composed of "shallow broken Iles," where it was very difficult to find fresh water. Smith departed to explore more of the Western Shore, where, after all, he would be more likely to find a northwestern passage.

Later that year, Smith's second Chesapeake expedition took him to the head of the bay, where he explored the Susquehanna River. He had no better luck there finding a route to the Pacific Ocean, but Smith did meet up with the Susquehannocks, whom he described as "giantlike" and "a mighty people," who arrived to greet him with "presents of venison, Tobacco pipes, Baskets, Targets, Bowes and Arrows" and in due course became trading partners to the English settlers. The rest of Smith's second expedition again focused on the bay's western shore.

The English did not revisit the Eastern Shore until 1613, when Captain Samuel Argoll returned with a somewhat better impression. He reported that its many islands had meadows where salt could be manufactured, and its small rivers could harbor boats and barges but not "ships of any great burthen." He also wrote, "Here also is a great store of fish, both shel-fish and other."

Folks struggling to make a living at Jamestown around this time probably became the first European settlers on the lower Eastern Shore, arriving by canoe and living there among friendly Native Americans. A census taken in 1624–25 listed forty-four males and seven females dispersed among nineteen houses. The authorities at Jamestown didn't exactly encourage these squatters, but they were willing to let them be. By 1632, the settlers on the lower Eastern Shore were documenting their own court proceedings.

Captain John Smith, one of the earliest explorers of the Eastern Shore. *Library of Congress.*

Authorities in England began addressing their decrees to "ye Colonie of Virginia, and ye Kingdome of Accawmacke," tacitly acknowledging that the Eastern Shore had a separate identity.

In the 1630s, an attempt to settle farther north on the Eastern Shore was made by an interesting person by the name of William Clayborne (sometimes spelled Claiborne). Clayborne must have had some pull in England, because the King of England nominated him for the council of Virginia's governor and appointed him as the colony's secretary of state. By 1631, he had a royal license to trade with other American plantations established by the English or the Dutch. At the time, there was no international or intercolonial trade being conducted in America, though enterprising individuals had discovered that the local aborigines were willing to give them in trade the pelts of various animals that could fetch a nice profit in Europe. Clayborne used his authority to establish two trading posts: one on the Eastern Shore on Kent Island (which was at the time thought to be a peninsula) and the other on Palmer's Island on the Western Shore near the mouth of the Susquehanna River.

What William Clayborne never had was an official land grant or permission to establish his own settlement. Nevertheless, in 1631, he sent a number of individuals to Kent Island, where they constructed a fort and, over the following several years, a church, a windmill and a shed to store peltry and the "truck" that the English used to barter with the Indians. Eventually, they established three plantations: one belonging to Clayborne, named Craford, and the others belonging to Clayborne's lieutenant and his brother-in-law.

In 1631, King Charles I signed a charter granting land north of Virginia to Sir George Calvert, or the first Lord Baltimore, a promising politician and practicing Catholic who was interested in both commercial opportunity and creating a refuge for English Catholics in the New World. Before this paperwork was officially concluded, George Calvert died, leaving the grant to his son Cecilius. Unlike Virginia, which had been colonized by a joint stock company, Maryland was set up as a proprietary colony in which its lord proprietor—that would be the Lord Baltimore—was free to grant land, establish courts and appoint judges and act more or less like a monarch, though he could not contravene established English law. The colony's name, Maryland, glorified not the Blessed Virgin Mary but England's queen, who was named Henrietta Maria. Maryland's first settlers arrived in 1634, under the command of Leonard Calvert, Cecilius's brother. They established the colony's capital on a broad, inviting inlet into the Potomac River and named the town St. Mary's City.

Maryland's charter stipulated that the colony occupied land lying between the Potomac's north shore and the fortieth degree of latitude, meaning that William Clayborne's various commercial operations were now officially located in Maryland. Clayborne argued that since he, a Virginian, had settled Kent Island and his upper bay trading post, these places had to remain in

Virginia. Clayborne rebelled against the jurisdiction of the Baltimore family. After several years of trying to work things out politically, Maryland's lord proprietor sent his brother Leonard Calvert to Kent Island with a military force. Once Leonard Calvert had successfully seized Clayborne's settlement, Cecilius gave it to him as a reward. Leonard then bestowed it on the Brent family, in whose hands it remained for generations.

Throughout the rest of the seventeenth century and into the early eighteenth century, Maryland's colonial government established its earliest counties, including those on the Eastern Shore, named Kent County, Talbot County, Somerset County and Dorchester County. Later subdivisions created the Eastern Shore counties named Cecil, Queen Anne's, Caroline, Wicomico and Worcester.

Down in Virginia, "ye Kingdome of Accawmacke" became one of eight shires into which that colony was divided in 1634. In 1642, Virginia's assembly adopted the name Northampton for this particular shire. There's no record of exactly when it happened, but Northampton Shire was later divided into Northampton and Accomack Counties.

The Eastern Shore Indians remained on the friendly side, selling their new English neighbors corn and pelts and making gifts of land. But many Indians succumbed to diseases to which they had no inherited immunity, and their survivors moved away, leaving only a few small and sparsely settled villages on the Eastern Shore at the beginning of the eighteenth century.

During the later seventeenth century and early eighteenth century, the Eastern Shore's population grew, and its counties required courthouses where litigants, lawyers and witnesses could resolve their differences. Sometimes a county seat would be established where a market or trading center already existed, as in the case of Somerset County's Princess Anne or Dorchester County's Cambridge. Talbot County constructed its first courthouse on an old Native American trail near a preexisting Quaker meetinghouse. Eastville became the place where courts convened in Virginia's Northampton County, and its circa 1732 courthouse still stands on Eastville's village green.

Similarly, transatlantic trade demanded official ports. In 1683, Maryland named Oxford in Talbot County a seaport, and the town became an international shipping center during the colonial period. Kent County's Chestertown became an important port for the export of tobacco and wheat around 1750. Chestertown has a historic district along its Water Street where several impressive residences dating from the mid- to late eighteenth century still stand, including the brick dwelling known as the Customs

The old colonial courthouse in Eastville, Virginia. *Author's collection.*

House, which is now owned by Washington College and sometimes open for tours. The size and stateliness of the dwellings suggest the prosperity this port enjoyed. In Oxford, which was likely the more important town, pretty much nothing is left from the port's colonial glory days.

Despite encouragement by both Maryland's and Virginia's colonial governments to establish them, other towns were slow to develop on the Eastern Shore. Taking their places were the growing de facto towns of its expanding plantations. The more prosperous plantations had their own wharves where ships and smaller vessels could dock. Surrounding the plantation owner's house were more modest dwellings for slaves, laborers and artisans, as well as facilities where anything the plantation dwellers needed, such as cloth, furniture, cart wheels, barrels and horseshoes, could be manufactured. In Maryland, many plantations were originally called manors, and their owners were technically lords and ladies, though formal titles had a way of disappearing in colonial America.

Generally, plantations lacked their own churches. To the twenty-first-century tourist, surviving colonial Eastern Shore churches can seem puzzlingly located in the middle of nowhere, but at the time they were constructed, they were probably centrally located among the various plantations where their congregants lived.

As a farm became established, its owner generally made improvements to his home. Early Eastern Shore dwellings were pretty basic, consisting of a single-room clapboard cottage with a chimney on one gable end and a simple loft. The owner could later add new sections or maybe convert the original single-room dwelling into a kitchen. Eventually, an Eastern Shore plantation house style evolved, incorporating a central hall running between the dwelling's front and rear doors, which gave access to other first-floor rooms and was connected to a second floor by a graceful staircase. Since the owner's most important visitors would be arriving by water, he tended to orient his house with the front façade facing a water landing, which was reached through a formal garden. Around back, there would be a drive connecting the house with a possibly quite distant public road.

Because both the population and the assets of the Eastern Shore were spread so thin, the region was only tangentially affected by the wars on American soil during the eighteenth and nineteenth centuries. In 1774,

The Eastern Shore's earliest settlers lived in houses like the Pear Valley Cottage. *Author's collection.*

after Chestertown received word that the British had closed the port of Boston, the locals who sympathized with Boston's Sons of Liberty drafted the Chestertown Resolves, stating that the British Parliament had acted unconstitutionally by subjecting the colonies to a tax on tea in a way that was "oppressive and calculated to enslave the Americans." Although it can be documented that a ship named the *Geddes* was in port that May, having arrived from Europe, there is no record to support the town's tradition that a group of men boarded the ship and threw tea into the Chester River, assuming that the *Geddes* even had any tea among its cargo. Nevertheless, the modern citizens of Chestertown have celebrated the so-called Chestertown Tea Party on Memorial Day weekend since 1976, with a parade, craft fair and waterfront events, including one called Toss the Tory.

In 1777, British general Howe landed his warships at what was then known as the Head of Elk, now Elkton, but Howe was just passing through. He marched north to fight the Battle of Brandywine in Pennsylvania and then to chase George Washington and the Continental army into winter quarters at Valley Forge while the British occupied Philadelphia.

The Chesapeake Bay saw a bit more excitement during the War of 1812, when the British occupied Tangier and Watts Islands, making Tangier Harbor the base for the invaders who would burn Washington, D.C., and bombard Baltimore. From time to time, raiding parties also encroached on Eastern Shore properties, but there were no large cities for them to destroy, and their seemingly halfhearted attempts were easily repulsed by the locals. For example, in May 1814, the British tried to land on the north side of Pungoteague Creek, but the local militia fought them off in what is known as the Battle of Rumley's Gut. In August of the same year, in the Battle of Caulk's Field, British came ashore north of Rock Hall to burn some barns and farmhouses, until they were again beaten back by local militia.

There's a legend that British raiders more or less surrendered to an Eastern Shore lady known as Catherine, or Kitty, Knight. After burning Fredericktown and lower Georgetown, they advanced uphill to set afire two brick houses located there. Kitty stamped out the flames and stood her ground, pleading with British admiral Cockburn himself, who then spared a church and several houses. Kitty later purchased one of the houses on the hill overlooking Georgetown and is said to still haunt the place, which had long operated as a restaurant and bed-and-breakfast called the Kitty Knight House. In 2018, it reopened under new management.

The Civil War plunged the Eastern Shore into an interesting position, since Delaware, Maryland and Virginia had all been slave states, but only

Virginia seceded from the Union. Eastern Shore Virginians who wanted to join the Confederate army had to sail across the bay, which Union forces had blockaded early in the war. Other Eastern Shore Virginians formed local militias to protect their homes and farms from Union boat landings.

Maryland stayed in the Union, but the loyalties of its population were very divided, and many cargo boats left Baltimore for Virginia's Eastern Shore, where blockade runners using smaller boats delivered their goods farther south. In 1861, the U.S. War Department decided to put a stop to this by literally invading the eastern shore of Virginia. Thousands of Federal soldiers gathered near the state line. Since the Virginia militia volunteers were equipped with nothing but their personal shotguns and old muskets, plus cannon left over from the War of 1812, they discreetly retreated as Union soldiers marched south in November 1861. Virginia's two Eastern Shore counties were officially joined to those of the newly organized Union state of West Virginia. Other than that, life went on pretty much as usual, with Eastern Shore residents conducting business with the cities of Baltimore, Philadelphia and New York, though all vessels had to be licensed and were prohibited from entering or leaving remote creeks at night.

The daily lives of Eastern Shore residents of the eighteenth and nineteenth centuries were probably less impacted by any war than by the gradual replacement of tobacco by corn and grains, and later truck farm produce, as the region's major crops, essentially ending its plantation economy. Sidney George Fisher, a Philadelphia lawyer who for a time owned Mount Harmon Plantation, still standing in Earleville, Maryland, left a detailed account of nineteenth-century Eastern Shore farm life in the diaries he kept from 1834 to 1871. He wrote about planting wheat, corn and timothy on his property, where he later added extensive fruit orchards.

But no matter what Fisher planted, anything he wanted to market rather than consume on his own plantation posed a transportation problem. A farmer had to get his surplus to the nearest port that had ferry service to a city market, either in his own small boat or in a wagon drawn by a horse or mule over poor roads. In 1850, Fisher commented, "If I can get a wharf built at my landing, it would be a great convenience there particularly if the [potential steamboat] line to Phila. should be started. It would certainly add much to the value and income of this property, which is well calculated for producing early vegetables and fruit and these are far more profitable than anything else. The difficulty is to get the wharf built."

In the decades following the Civil War, technology was transforming life in most of the rest of America, but life on the Eastern Shore took on its time

Sidney George Fisher might have sat here contemplating the creeks surrounding Mount Harmon Plantation. *Author's collection.*

capsule quality. Some visitors, like Howard Pyle, found it amusing. Others found it charming. In a book published in 1884 about vacation cruising in the Delaware and Chesapeake Bays, author J.T. Rothrock commented, "When we say that on the Eastern Shore one finds more traces of the old colonial life and customs than elsewhere in Maryland, no disparagement is intended."

Some remnants of the old plantation economy survived through the twentieth century. The mansion house at Sidney George Fisher's Mount Harmon suffered fire, ruin and neglect during the later nineteenth and early twentieth centuries, until a descendant of the man who had bought it and lived there in the later years of the eighteenth century purchased it in 1963. Mrs. Henry Boden IV planned to restore it to what she imagined was its splendor during her ancestors' residence. What she ended up with was more Colonial Revival than colonial, the mansion's furnishings reflecting her own taste for the flamboyant, with an emphasis on chinoiserie. Today, Mount Harmon houses the late Mrs. Boden's collection of antiques from the Jacobean, Queen Anne, Chippendale and Federal periods made in

America, England, Ireland, Scotland and the Isle of Man. The rooms are crammed with far more furniture than the typical eighteenth-century planter would have possessed.

If you're not wowed by this fabulous collection of antiques, you'll certainly be impressed by the modifications Mrs. Boden added in efforts to make a colonial house livable in the twentieth century. Off of two of its bedrooms are modern bathrooms concealed by drapery, both equipped with sunken tiled tubs. One tub even has marble steps and a railing. Both bathroom areas have enormous marble sinks with custom faucets. The bathroom areas and the house's kitchen are decked out in colors popular in the 1960s: aqua, avocado green and lavender.

Mrs. Boden left her house to a national preservation organization with the idea that it be made open to visitors. It is now administered by the Friends of Mount Harmon, which sponsors its annual events celebrating colonial and Eastern Shore heritage. When we visited in 2014, the group's latest capital project was the reconstruction of a colonial-era smokehouse. It has since added replica slave quarters.

In Onancock, Virginia, the Eastern Shore of Virginia Historical Society, which manages Ker Place, seems to be trying to get away from excessive romanticizing of the plantation past. Ker Place was constructed between 1799 and 1803 in the Georgian style, which was by that time giving way to the Federal period in architectural history. Ker Place belonged to a plantation owner named John Shepherd Ker and his wife, Agnes Corbin Ker. It had been restored to its presumed appearance circa 1806 using a household inventory for that date. When we visited in 2014, the society had transformed the mansion's upstairs rooms into exhibit space, mounting an exhibit of hand-sewn period bed hangings and draperies made by a volunteer sewing guild. Our guide mentioned that the society has been changing its strategic direction from interpreting Ker Place as a house museum frozen in time to a venue for history-themed activities of interest to the surrounding community. That summer, the society had plans for lectures about the Civil War and Reconstruction. It was also coordinating an event where a replica ship called the *Godspeed* would be arriving at the town wharf to illustrate the experience of crossing the Atlantic to the New World in the early seventeenth century.

Actual remains of the Eastern Shore's seventeenth century are harder to find. Between 1988 and 1994, archaeologists and architectural historians discovered and excavated the foundations of Arlington, a mansion built around 1670 by the Custis family on Old Plantation Creek about four miles south of the town of Cape Charles City in Virginia. When it was constructed, it would have been a large rectangular brick building two rooms wide and two rooms deep with four chimneys, easily the most impressive dwelling not only on the Eastern Shore but also in the colony of Virginia, if not all the British colonies.

When we visited in the summer of 2014, we found some traces of Arlington's footprint in an overgrown field, identifiable only with the help of historic markers. A short stroll away, we found a tiny brick cemetery and the final resting places of two of Arlington's early owners: John Custis II and John Custis IV.

In 1903, a couple of historians set out to find the site of William Clayborne's settlement on Kent Island, known as Kent Fort Manor, and they recorded their experience in an article published in a periodical titled the *Johns Hopkins University Studies in Historical and Political Science*. In 1837, an earlier historian, John Leeds Bozman, had written a political history of Maryland in which he recorded that Kent Fort had been built on a slight elevation on the bank of the first navigable creek on the island's eastern side above its southern point. The twentieth-century historians set out to find this spot, describing their journey from Kent Island's main town, Stephensville, along "an excellent country road through level fertile country with interesting old farm houses standing at a distance." The road finally ended at a gate. A man living in a nearby house told them they had indeed reached Kent Fort Manor and led them to the spot where tradition proclaimed the Clayborne settlement had once stood. There the historians found "a number of fragments of glazed bricks about seventy yards from the shore," which might or might not have been part of an early Eastern Shore manor house.

A little over a century later, in the summer of 2014, my husband, Mat, and I decided to see if we could follow in their footsteps, or rather carriage wheel ruts. We had an advantage lacking in the early twentieth century, namely, a Google map that did identify a point near the southern tip of Kent Island as Kent Fort Manor, so we set out from the town that people now spell as Stevensville along the country road now called Route 8, or Romancoke Road. Stay on Romancoke Road, and you'll end up in the community called Romancoke, where the road ends at a public boat launch and community park. To get to the place that Google identified as Kent Fort Manor, we had to make a dog-leg turn onto Kent Point Road.

Immediately, the property values jumped from an average of about $300,000 to close to $1 million or more. We located Kent Fort Lane, a shaded, gravel-topped, one-lane road with several mailboxes at its intersection with

Kent Point Road, indicating the presence of secluded abodes. We could see the sparkling bay through the trees that lined this lane, and our map did show that it ran north of an inlet called Scaffold Creek, which might have been the navigable creek Bozman had described. However, according to Google, this lane did not lead to Kent Fort Manor.

We later learned that the spot where Google wanted to lead us, on the east side of Kent Point Road a little south of Kent Fort Lane, was more or less the former location of a small frame house with a steeply pitched roof, one and a half stories high and one room deep, that for a long time had been thought to be the original manor house constructed in the late 1630s at William Clayborne's settlement. A historian named Henry Chandlee Forman had said so in his 1934 book titled *Early Manor and Plantation Houses of Maryland*. But he retracted that opinion in a later book and suggested an early nineteenth-century date for this structure. Further research is no longer possible because the little house was demolished in 1964.

A little farther down Kent Point Road we noticed a property enclosed by a fence with a large house at the end of a long drive lined with trees. It happened to be up for sale at an asking price of $849,000. A sign at the end of the driveway proclaimed this to be "Kent Fort Manor, circa 1639," but one did not have to be an architectural historian to realize that the buildings on this property were much newer than that. Just like the no longer extant little frame house, this place had apparently derived its name and its pedigree from an old land grant. Unlike the early twentieth-century historians, we found no presumed remains of the old structures, but the excursion did illustrate how the physical artifacts of the past become inexorably obliterated.

It was our trip to Mount Harmon that most clearly evoked the Eastern Shore of the mid- to late nineteenth century and gave us a real understanding of the dilemma facing farmers like Sidney George Fisher—not our tour of the mansion but rather the effort of getting there. After driving four miles west of Cecilton through farmland, we finally reached the property's entrance. Then we drove another two miles on a one-lane dirt and gravel road through a tunnel of overhanging Osage orange trees. Finally, we reached the mansion, which was located on a peninsula extending into the Sassasfras River, a spot that was identified on early maps as "World's End."

It was a pleasant enough drive, but I just had to ask our guide what happens when one meets a vehicle proceeding in the opposite direction. She informed us that somebody has to back up until they reach one of the few places on the lane wide enough for two cars to pass each other.

It was a lesson in just how isolated and remote an Eastern Shore plantation once could be. Sophisticated authors of the late nineteenth century, like Pyle and Rothrock, might find the resulting way of life amusing or charming, but the farmers and fishermen who wanted to make a buck, and the gourmets who wanted to consume their products, desperately needed a solution.

2

Modern Transportation Comes to the Delmarva

In 1818, Samuel Breck, then Philadelphia's state senator, published a pamphlet defending the reputation of his state, Pennsylvania, and predicting a rosy future for the commerce of Philadelphia. He began, "We listen with patience to the New-England, New-York, and Maryland writers, whose praises on their own doings, rise, not unfrequently, to the most exalted panegyric." He added that those same accounts were often accompanied by the "side-blows at poor Pennsylvania" but concluded that Pennsylvania's planned and already accomplished "internal improvements" would keep the commonwealth competitive.

The early years of the American republic witnessed intense competition among the states for development of their ports and supporting inland transportation projects that folks collectively referred to as internal improvements. Through the late eighteenth century, Philadelphia had remained America's most important port, its trade based on the export of grain to the West Indies and Europe. After Philadelphia lost its lead to New York between 1810 and 1820, entrepreneurs built a system of canals linking Philadelphia with Reading far up the Schuylkill River and the Schuylkill River with the Susquehanna. New York had increased its foreign trade, instituted a regular transatlantic packet and developed business along the Atlantic coast, particularly bringing up cotton from the South for export to Europe. The planned construction of the Erie Canal then promised to foster New York City's relationship with the American interior. During the same years, Baltimore grew rapidly, exporting grain and tobacco grown in Virginia and Maryland, as well as agricultural products from central Pennsylvania that reached this city via improvements on the Susquehanna River.

Farther south, Norfolk had been founded in the 1630s as a land grant to the Thorowgood family on the west side of the mouth of the Lynnhaven River. Norfolk had developed as a livestock ranch, trading cattle, sheep and hogs with the West Indies. By 1636, the Thorowgoods had established a ferry between Norfolk and Portsmouth on the Elizabeth River, as well as a few roads and cart trails south, where forests of oak, pine and cypress offered a trade in lumber, tar and pitch. In the early to mid-eighteenth century, once local pirates like Blackbeard had been eliminated from the area, Norfolk had thrived as a port, adding flour to its export trade of products from the surrounding area, by then including North Carolina, to the West Indies.

Before the official start of the American Revolution, the British burned Norfolk, and during the war, it was seized and its vessels and naval stores captured, while its civilian population was plagued by plundering Tory gangs, until Lord Cornwallis surrendered at nearby Yorktown in 1781. Norfolk's waterfront began making a comeback in the early nineteenth century, but the town suffered anew with the nation's embargo on overseas trade leading up to the War of 1812.

Norfolk's business prospects greatly improved in 1814 and 1815, with the completion of the Dismal Swamp Canal linking the Elizabeth River with North Carolina's Albemarle Sound. The canal soon became an important inland waterway, as it was widened and developed in the ensuing years, enabling Norfolk and Portsmouth to develop as export ports for agricultural products. By the end of the 1830s, ships were sailing from Norfolk to Baltimore, Philadelphia, New York and Boston.

During the same time period, traveling overland remained tedious at best. One could travel by stagecoach between New York and Philadelphia and then south along a route that meandered through Darby, Chester, Wilmington and Newark to Baltimore, but the hilly terrain in this area made for a rough journey. Stages left Baltimore for Washington, crossing the Patapsco via ferry, but the roads along this route improved only as one neared the capital.

On the eastern shore of the Chesapeake Bay, one could head south from the head of the Elk River in Maryland, where the town of Elkton had become a county seat, and over a road to a port called Rock Hall, where ferries crossed the Chesapeake Bay to Annapolis. But to get to Rock Hall, travelers had to take ferries across two other rivers, the Bohemia and the Sassafras.

The federal government briefly ventured into public road building after the United States government opened the Ohio territory for settlement in 1806. Congress appropriated money for the construction of a road that would reach and run through Ohio, known as the National Road or National Pike, or sometimes the Cumberland Road, for the town of Cumberland, Maryland, where the road commenced. By 1818, the road had been constructed as far west as Wheeling, but by then, the nation was still dealing with the expenses of the War of 1812, and its leaders had turned against federally subsidized transportation projects, leaving subsequent overland improvements to the states and private enterprise.

The early nineteenth century was also a time when Americans were debating the relative advantages of three different systems of internal improvements: roads, including private toll roads called turnpikes, versus canals versus the new technology of railroading. Since the Delmarva Peninsula lacked a major Atlantic port below Wilmington, its earliest internal improvements included one of each, all located roughly where the peninsula was narrowest, and all intended to link the ports of Philadelphia and Baltimore.

After 1816, travelers could use a turnpike road between the Delaware River port known as New Castle and Frenchtown Wharf on the Elk River, an Eastern Shore port town that had been considered important enough to invite a British raid in 1813. The earliest steamboats to ply the Chesapeake Bay had sailed from Frenchtown Wharf to Baltimore.

In 1824, construction began on the massive Chesapeake and Delaware (C&D) Canal, a project promoted more by Philadelphia merchants than those of Maryland or Delaware. When the canal was completed in 1829, passengers and freight could be loaded on a steamboat in Philadelphia in the morning and be in Baltimore by nightfall of the same day.

In 1827, Maryland's assembly authorized the New Castle and Frenchtown Turnpike Company to build a railroad on or near its turnpike, assuming Delaware would allow trains to continue into that state, which did not happen until 1829. The railroad road bed was constructed just south of the turnpike and parallel to it, terminating on a wharf on the Elk River just below the Frenchtown landing. The sixteen-mile railroad was completed in February 1832. Horses drew its freight cars and fairly commodious passenger cars, until its first steam locomotive arrived from England that August. The locomotive had been shipped in pieces and was assembled in New Castle under the direction of Matthias Baldwin, who would eventually become famous as a locomotive engine manufacturer in Philadelphia. The new locomotive pulled its first passenger train on September 10, 1832, making the New Castle and Frenchtown Rail Road one of America's earliest

The Chesapeake and Delaware Canal, completed in 1829. This bridge spans the canal in Chesapeake City, Maryland. *Author's collection.*

to offer steam-drawn scheduled passenger trains. The railroad advertised that trains left New Castle as soon as the Union Line steamboat arrived from Philadelphia and deposited passengers at a location where another steamboat from the same line stood waiting to take them to Baltimore. It evolved that larger freight cargoes continued to be generally shipped via the C&D Canal to avoid this boat-rail-boat transfer.

In his diaries, Sidney George Fisher mentioned that the New Castle and Frenchtown Rail Road made it possible for him to leave Philadelphia at seven o'clock in the morning and get to his Mount Harmon plantation around half past one. In Frenchtown, he could catch a steamboat heading south for Fredericktown and Georgetown, or he could board the steamer bound for Baltimore if its captain was willing to put him ashore at a place called Ford's Landing.

In 1838, Sidney George Fisher heard that the New Castle and Frenchtown Rail Road might extend a branch south from some point on its line to the mouth of the Sassafras River. This would eliminate his need to board a steamboat in Frenchtown en route to his plantation and would

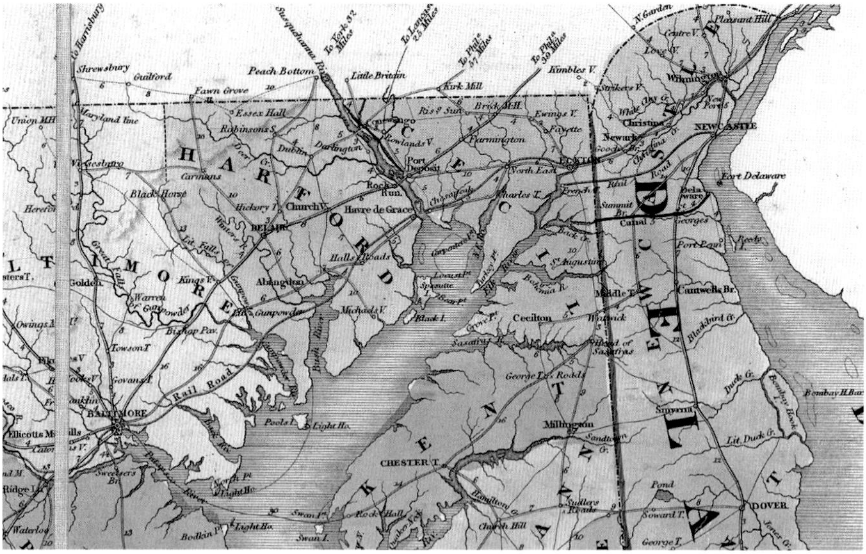

This map, drawn in 1839, shows the route of the New Castle and Frenchtown Rail Road, the C&D Canal and roads of the upper Eastern Shore. *Library of Congress, Geography and Map Division.*

generally make north–south transportation easier for those then forced to use the ramshackle road from Elkton to Rock Hall. It would also increase property values. He wrote, "[The railroad] would necessarily pass within a quarter of a mile of my entrance gate, would add much to the value of the farm, and enable me to come down with great ease and at all seasons in four or five hours." The proposed project also showed that by that time, a quest was already on for new ways to link Philadelphia with points farther south than Baltimore.

As early as 1824, the Philadelphia, Dover and Norfolk Steamboat and Transportation Company offered passengers steamboat service from Philadelphia to a landing north of Dover, where passengers and baggage were transferred to stagecoaches for an overland journey to Seaford, where other steamboats continued down the Nanticoke River across the Chesapeake Bay to Norfolk. Unfortunately, the company was undercapitalized for such ambitious plans, and service was discontinued after little more than a year.

In 1833, Maryland granted a charter to the Eastern Shore Railroad Company, which planned a railroad from Elkton south to Tangier Sound, where steamboats were also intended to connect with Norfolk. By this time, Virginia's Portsmouth and Roanoke Railroad had been incorporated and would soon be able to make connections between Norfolk and western

Virginia and points even farther south. It took Maryland until 1835 to provide a $1 million subsidy for the proposed railroad, and the following year, its 118-mile route was surveyed.

In 1836, the State of Delaware granted a charter to the Delaware Railroad Company to construct a railroad running north and south through Delaware in the general direction of Cape Charles, with branches running east and west to Delaware port towns like Lewes and Seaford. To reach Cape Charles, tracks would have to be laid through Maryland, but the railroad's promoters thought that Marylanders would eventually go along. Even if they didn't, the railroad could still provide access to the Chesapeake, and therefore Norfolk, through Seaford, and the railroad would still connect the farms of Delaware's Kent and Sussex Counties with markets in Wilmington and Philadelphia.

The nationwide financial crisis known as the Panic of 1837 stalled both the Eastern Shore and Delaware Railroad projects. A major recession lasted into the 1840s, causing budget and funding problems for most states, while widespread pessimism caused private investment for internal improvements from banks and individuals to dry up.

Thanks mainly to the lobbying efforts of Delaware's chief justice Samuel M. Harrington, the dormant Delaware Railroad was rechartered by Delaware's house and senate in 1849. Once again, the goal was a connection with Norfolk, and the railroad's contemplated route was much the same as that of the defunct Philadelphia, Dover and Norfolk Steamboat and Transportation Company, with trains replacing the stagecoaches. In his speech delivered on March 6, 1852, to mark the opening of subscriptions for the railroad, Harrington stated, "The Delaware Railroad, contemplated by the foregoing charter, is to connect the cities of Philadelphia and Norfolk, in a direct line of travel and transportation. The natural facilities are such as are afforded by no other route; there being two bays and rivers stretching in a direct line, and requiring only about forty-three miles of railway, over level country, to unite them."

But an editorial published in the *Delaware Gazette* that same year indicated that people were also talking about reviving the original 1830s plans for the railroad: "We intend when we have more leisure and space, to say something about the practicability and propriety of a connection of the Delaware Railroad with that of the New Castle and its [the Delaware Railroad's] extension down the peninsula to Cherrystone opposite Norfolk, so as to bring most of the Southern travel from Philadelphia, New York and Boston through this way, as well as much produce from that country." By "the New Castle" the editor meant not merely the old New Castle and Frenchtown Rail Road but also its new eastern extension, the New Castle and Wilmington Railroad, which had been completed that same year by another railroad company called the Philadelphia, Wilmington and Baltimore Railroad (PWB), which had acquired the New Castle and Frenchtown Rail Road in 1839.

Conceived as a link between three important cities in three different states, the PWB was originally chartered as four separate railroads in the 1830s. Its continuous route between Philadelphia and Baltimore opened in 1838, and by 1840, the separate railroad companies were officially merged. PWB survived its own brushes with bankruptcy during the 1840s and, by 1850, had emerged as a dependable carrier between two port cities and a major contributor to the growth of manufacturing in Wilmington.

PWB investors recognized the advantage to their own operations of having a north–south line through Delaware, and in June 1853, they effectively took control of the yet unbuilt Delaware Railroad. At a shareholders' meeting, several PWB executives joined the Delaware Railroad's board of directors, though Harrington remained railroad president. A chief engineer was appointed to make the final surveys. Delaware's legislature had already authorized the PWB and its New Castle and Frenchtown Rail Road to own the new railroad's stock and guarantee its bonds. In 1855, the PWB formally leased the Delaware Railroad.

By 1856, the Delaware Railroad had constructed actual trackage linking a town called Porter on the route of the old New Castle and Frenchtown Rail Road with the state capital of Dover and the port of Seaford. By 1859, the railroad's tracks reached a spot on the state line between Delaware and Maryland appropriately named Delmar. The railroad's headquarters was located just west of the town of Smyrna at a place named Clayton, after John M. Clayton, a Delaware politician and railroad promoter.

Once it became clear that the Delaware Railroad had solid backing, would indeed be constructed and could form the first segment in an efficient land-water route from Philadelphia to Norfolk and the South, the Delaware Railroad spawned the beginning of an entire network of short line feeder railroads running east and west from its north–south spine to the larger towns of Delaware and Maryland's eastern shore.

The earliest attempt to build an east–west feeder connecting with the Delaware Railroad was the Maryland and Delaware Railroad chartered in 1854 in Maryland and 1857 in Delaware. Its chief promoter was Tench Tilghman, grandson of a Revolutionary War hero of the same name. The Tilghman family had long been prominent in Maryland political and social circles, and they owned a large estate near Oxford. Born in 1810, Tench Tilghman had graduated from West Point in 1832 and served in the U.S. Army before returning to plantation life in Maryland.

In December 1856, the *Easton Gazette* reported on groundbreaking ceremonies for the Maryland and Delaware Railroad at Easton, during which Tench Tilghman was formally elected president of the young railroad by its stockholders. Many folks turned out for a procession from town to a meadow, where a gentleman named Dr. S. Harper, who had participated in groundbreaking ceremonies for the B&O Railroad in 1828, threw the first shovelful of earth before officials laid a cornerstone for future railroad buildings. In his speech, Tilghman said that the railroad's route had been surveyed, and grading was already completed in Delaware. He exhorted all citizens, especially large landowners, to invest.

The newspaper's coverage hinted at some earlier local controversy about this project. Perhaps the reporter was referring to the letter from an anonymous visitor from Philadelphia, which had appeared in the newspaper that September. The writer had declared himself amazed at the "imaginary obstacles thrown in the way of this enterprise by certain old fogies in Talbot [County] who would have been behind the times, had they lived in the tenth century."

In June of the following year, the *Easton Gazette* reported that "the last section of the road between Hillsborough and the State line, will be finished in a few weeks." By 1859, the line was graded and its bridges constructed as far as Greensborough in Maryland, and citizens were debating whether the railroad should terminate in Easton or Oxford. Typically, support for the ongoing project was strongest during the winter. In February 1858, the *Easton Gazette* editorialized, "Let us have a rail road then, so that when we are hemmed in by the ice—as we have been for several winters past, and almost to the exclusion of the necessaries of life—we can go to and fro without having to take the cold and disagreeable stage route."

Its promoters had hoped the Maryland and Delaware Railroad would be completed by 1862, but construction was interrupted by the Civil War and did not resume until October 1865. As workmen laying rails and ties actually approached Easton, a faction of citizens who did not want the railroad tracks extending into the center of town prevailed, and the railroad was constructed to just skirt Easton to the east—until the town grew out to meet and surround its depots and rail yard. By 1869, trains were running to Easton, which remained the end of the line until 1871, when the railroad was completed to Oxford.

In 1856, the Queen Anne and Kent Railroad was chartered to serve the two eastern shore counties mentioned in its name. One terminus was planned for Centreville, the county seat of Queen Anne County, but there was some controversy about where the railroad would go. Suggestions for its other terminus included Fredericktown or Elkton before the Civil War and Galena via Crumpton, or Massey's Cross Roads via Millington, when the project was resumed in 1866. The Delaware Railroad's managers more or less made the decision for the promoters of the Queen Anne and Kent in 1867, when they constructed the Townsend Branch Railroad from Townsend to Massey's Cross Roads (now called Massey). In 1868, rail service began to Centreville, where the tracks ended at Centreville Landing on a branch of the Corsica River. Freight hauling continued for years, but because the railroad was never extended to a better port, it never made much profit.

The Delaware Railroad lent a helping hand to the Dorchester and Delaware Railroad by constructing a spur called the Dorchester Branch from Seaford to the state line. Chartered in 1866 in Maryland and 1867 in Delaware, the Dorchester and Delaware Railroad was intended to connect the ports of Seaford and Cambridge, which was then the largest town on the eastern shore of Maryland. Although the Delaware Railroad had to lend the Dorchester and Delaware money to complete construction, unlike the Queen Anne and Kent, this railroad was profitable from the day it opened in 1869, hauling passengers, as well as agricultural products, timber and seafood.

The Junction and Breakwater Railroad Company was incorporated in 1857 to connect the Delaware Railroad ultimately with the Delaware Breakwater in Lewes but more importantly with Milford, Delaware's largest town south of Wilmington, whose citizens had not been happy about being bypassed and forced to use a muddy stage road to get to the nearest train station. Milford had rail service as of August 25, 1859. In the beginning of September, the *Easton Gazette* reported, "Hundreds of citizens are said to have been at the depot to witness the arrival of the first locomotive, and the shrill whistle of which, put the town in a perfect commotion." Contractors then laid the last rail and spiked its joint. Chief engineer Tench F. Tilghman, described as "quite a young man," then delivered a speech. Because the Civil War intervened, the railroad was not completed to Lewes until 1869. It was extended to the resort town of Rehoboth Beach in 1878.

During the 1870s, the reach of the Junction and Breakwater Railroad was extended farther south by means of other railroads. The Breakwater and Frankford Railroad, completed in 1874, connected with the Junction and

Breakwater in Georgetown, Delaware, and then ran south to the state line, where the Worcester Rail Road, completed in 1876, ran through Maryland and Virginia to Franklin City on the Chincoteague Bay. From there, steamboats could take passengers to rustic Chincoteague or other ports on the Atlantic. In 1883, the three cooperating railroads were merged into the Delaware, Maryland and Virginia Railroad Company.

Chartered in 1856, the same year as the Queen Anne and Kent Railroad, the Kent County Rail Road is often confused with it, no doubt in part because it shared a terminus at Massey's Cross Roads, which was also its Delaware Railroad connection. Construction did not begin until 1869. The railroad was planned to run through Kennedyville and Worton to wharf facilities in Chestertown and then through Fairlee to Rock Hall's harbor on the Chesapeake Bay, which happened to be the Eastern Shore port geographically closest to Baltimore. In August 1870, the *Cecil Whig* reported that the line had been completed to Worton, and business was already good. By the end of the year, it was expected that the railroad would be completed to Chestertown.

By this time in railroading history, certain entrepreneurs were attempting to build railroad monopolies and empires covering long distances. Jay Gould, a speculator and railroad developer who has since been vilified by historians as the quintessential robber baron, had visions of a transportation route from New York to Baltimore across New Jersey, the Delaware Bay, the Delmarva Peninsula and the Chesapeake Bay. In 1873, Gould took control of the Kent County Rail Road, as well as two New Jersey railroads, and began construction of the Smyrna and Delaware Bay Railroad from the Delaware Bay to the Delaware-Maryland state line.

Gould's grand vision quickly succumbed to the financial Panic of 1873, but as a result of his wheeling and dealing, in 1877, the New Jersey Southern Railroad purchased the Kent County Rail Road and later merged it with the Smyrna and Delaware Bay Railroad into the Baltimore and Delaware Bay Railroad, the new name reflecting a new plan for a trans-Delmarva line linked to New Jersey. For a little while, this system drew some freight traffic in produce away from the Delaware Railroad, but its freight trains were seasonal. Regular service was available only between Clayton and Chestertown. The Baltimore and Delaware Bay Railroad remained under control of the New Jersey Southern's successor, the Central Railroad of New Jersey, until 1900 and outside the Delaware Railroad's emerging feeder empire.

Meanwhile, the Delaware Railroad's parent company, the Philadelphia, Wilmington and Baltimore Railroad, had become part of a longer route between New York and Washington, D.C., that was strategically important to two larger railroads. The B&O Railroad had used PWB tracks to serve passengers and freight heading to Philadelphia ever since the PWB opened. After the Pennsylvania Railroad completed its Baltimore and Potomac branch in 1873, it also ran trains over the PWB main line. The PWB's competent management had always kept its physical plant well maintained while also providing hefty dividends for its stockholders, and thus the PWB became a prize keenly coveted by both the Pennsy and the B&O.

In 1880, John W. Garrett of the B&O Railroad decided to distance his railroad from the Pennsy and compete more directly with it. The B&O had customarily sent trains across New Jersey to a terminal with ferries crossing to New York City via the tracks of the United New Jersey Railroad and Canal Company. But in 1871, the Pennsy leased the United New Jersey Railroad and Canal Company for a term of 999 years—in other words, forever. In December 1880, Garrett announced that B&O service from Philly to New York City would run over the so-called Bound Brook Route, or tracks controlled by the Reading Railroad and the Central Railroad of New Jersey.

This might have caused a few headaches for the PWB, because in January 1881, the PWB director's minute book records that a committee was formed to meet with a similar PRR committee "to endeavor to affect some arrangements under which the losses now caused by the disputes between the B&O RR Co. and the PRR in respect to through business may be saved."

In February 1881, the Central Railroad of New Jersey announced that Jay Gould had been elected to its board. This was the same Jay Gould who just a few years before had tried to incorporate the tiny Kent County Rail Road into a prospective New York to Baltimore rail and water route. It seemed that this dream had yet to die. Perhaps not coincidentally, on February 24, 1881, the PWB appointed to its own board Robert Garrett (John W. Garrett's son) and George G. Haven of the Central Railroad of New Jersey.

The management team at the Pennsylvania Railroad would have been blind or negligent not to suspect that some sort of collusion between the Garretts and Gould, for the purpose of competing with the Pennsy's D.C. to New York business, was about to happen if it had not already taken place. Indeed, the Pennsy's ailing and outgoing president, Thomas A. Scott, warned the prospective new president, George Roberts, not to trust John Garrett and to expect a challenge. He suggested that Roberts rely on one Alexander J. Cassatt, whom Scott had mentored. Cassatt had also been the man who had handled the negotiations for the Pennsy's long-term lease of the United New Jersey Railroad and Canal Company.

One way that Garrett and the B&O could seriously stymie the Pennsy would be to buy the Philadelphia, Wilmington and Baltimore Railroad and deny the Pennsy use of its tracks between Philadelphia and Baltimore—or charge them outrageously for the privilege. Another would be to build a new rail line between Philadelphia and Baltimore and offer better and faster service on the longer haul between D.C. and New York City. But both of these options would cost a lot of money, and the B&O lacked sufficient resources to go it alone.

Regardless of what was going on in the head of John Garrett, his own railroad briefly became a target in someone else's moneymaking scheme. Described by his biographer as a "railroad adventurer," Colonel Henry S. McComb had been buying up shares in the Delaware Western Railroad since 1879. The Delaware Western existed only on paper—that is, it had been chartered by the State of Delaware but never actually constructed, and McComb's purchases made it seem like he was preparing to build a rival to the PWB. Or perhaps he just wanted to get the larger and richer railroads that depended on the PWB to buy him out. In March 1880, McComb met with Thomas Scott and George Roberts of the Pennsy, who apparently failed to take the bait. Yet when McComb later approached Robert Garrett of the B&O and William H. Vanderbilt of the New York Central Railroad, who wanted to extend his own lines into Pennsylvania, they put together a syndicate including Jay Gould and other investors to fund construction of the Delaware Western.

When the upper house of Delaware's legislature passed a bill expanding the charter privileges of the not-yet-existent Delaware Western Railroad, those capitalists who were invested in the PWB were convinced that the threat of impending competition to their railroad was real. Most of these investors lived in Boston, and the largest of them was an investment banker named Nathaniel Thayer. Thayer came up with a plan to sell a controlling interest in the PWB to the Garrett/Gould/Vanderbilt syndicate and thus make it unnecessary for them to build a competing line. On February 17, 1881, the syndicate agreed to purchase 120,000 shares of PWB stock at seventy dollars per share, a price Thayer assured them a sufficient number of PWB investors would agree to.

As news leaked out, a reporter from the *Philadelphia Inquirer* approached Isaac Hinckley, president of the PWB. In an account published on February 23, headlined "Absorbed," the reporter quoted Hinckley: "I know but little as yet in regard to the details. Today I received a telegram of four or five lines from Mr. Thayer, of Boston, one of the largest stockholders in the

P., W. and B., stating that he had sold his stock to Robert Garrett, third vice president of the Baltimore and Ohio, and a broker by the name of Haven, I think. They have also secured other stock sufficient to give them a controlling interest."

The *Philadelphia Inquirer* also sought reaction from the Pennsylvania Railroad. The unnamed "prominent official" who had been interviewed expressed some surprise, noting that Mr. Hinckley had been at the PRR office the previous day for a conference and insisted that he had no knowledge that Nathaniel Thayer had sold his stock to anyone. The PRR official added, "If necessary we could build our own line to Baltimore, and for this purpose it would only be necessary to lay sixty miles of tracks." Asked whether the new PWB management might "injure or delay" PRR traffic, the Pennsy official replied, "If the new operators choose to be ugly they can, but it is not always well to do so."

The syndicate apparently anticipated the Pennsy's response. Early in March, the *Baltimore Sun* reported, "The Pennsylvania Railroad was consulted, however, by the syndicate, and being brought into the negotiation by the Thayer party, were offered a place in the syndicate because it was not desirable that the Pennsylvania Road should build its own line across the country to this city." The syndicate offered the PRR a one-third interest in the deal. Alexander J. Cassatt was probably the official who said no at a meeting held February 19. The March 11 edition of the *Railroad Gazette* was able to confirm that Cassatt had been in New York City that day.

Despite Thayer's assurances, a number of PWB investors thought seventy dollars per share was too low, and they did not like the fact that Garrett and Haven were already on the board and apparently in position to take over. These dissidents formed a committee, and on March 4, the *Railroad Gazette* reported they had signed powers of attorney to sell or transfer their stock. By March 9, the *Baltimore Sun* reported that said committee consisted of five gentlemen who collectively owned over half of PWB. Henry P. Kidder of Kidder, Peabody & Co. headed the committee and was already in contact with "officers of the Pennsylvania Railroad Company," essentially inviting the Pennsy to offer them more for their shares.

In July 1901, a periodical called the *World's Work*, which covered American business and world affairs, included an article about Alexander J. Cassatt by Francis Barksdale, with an account of a very interesting meeting between Robert Garrett and George Roberts that occurred around this time, including its dialog. At the time the article was published, Roberts had passed away, and Cassatt was president of the Pennsylvania Railroad, so it's likely that the author based his article solely on what he learned from an interview with Cassatt.

It seems that once Robert Garrett thought his syndicate had a deal and that he had control of the PWB, he visited Roberts in his office to tell him so, adding, possibly in sarcastic tones, "We are not disposed, however, to disturb your relations with the property, and you need not give yourself any uneasiness on that score." In the article, Roberts, "in his dry manner," expressed surprise that the deal had moved so far along and immediately went to confer with Cassatt. The article also implied that it had been Cassatt who the renegade PWB investors had been in touch with.

When the telegrams going back and forth convinced both Kidder and the PRR that a deal could be made, Cassatt and Roberts, together with other PRR officials, went to New York to meet with the PWB committee at the Brevoort House hotel. After seven hours of negotiation, it was agreed that the committee would deliver to the Pennsy a majority of outstanding stock on July 1 at seventy-eight dollars per share. The same price would be offered to all PWB shareholders who cared to sell by the same date.

The deal was concluded at midnight, just before March 8, which was the annual scheduled PRR shareholders' meeting. Roberts telegraphed a call for a special meeting of PRR directors that morning and requested board approval "for the purchase of a control of the capital stock of the Philadelphia, Wilmington and Baltimore Railroad Company," noting that they had signed and witnessed agreements with five PWB investors for the purchase of ninety-two thousand shares. The PRR board unanimously voted yes.

Later that day, when the shareholders gathered and following their approval of the PRR annual report for the previous year, Roberts announced the real news, saying, "I desire to call the attention of the shareholders to the fact that the Philadelphia, Wilmington and Baltimore road has passed into the control of the Pennsylvania Railroad, and the necessary steps have been taken to carry out the contract." The *Baltimore Sun* reported on March 9, "This was received with an outburst of cheers." The stockholders unanimously approved the deal, and the meeting erupted in yet more cheering and applause. By the end of the month, Roberts and Cassatt were able to purchase 217,819 shares of the PWB's existing 235,901 shares.

It appears that one of the Pennsy's first objectives was to get Garrett and Haven off the PWB board. On April 21, Garrett sent a one-sentence letter to PWB's president and directors stating, "I hereby beg to tender my resignation as a member of your board." His resignation was quickly accepted, and by summer, PRR executives were suggesting replacements for PWB board vacancies and other positions on Pennsy letterhead where the words "Pennsylvania Railroad Company" were crossed out by hand and replaced with the name of the Philadelphia, Wilmington and Baltimore Railroad. Among others, they suggested that Alexander J. Cassatt be elected to the board. Garrett's syndicate dissolved, and the B&O was forced to buy McComb's Delaware Western Railroad charter and start building its own line to Philadelphia to run trains to New York independent of the Pennsy, while paying the Pennsy fees in the meantime.

George Brooke Roberts was PRR president when the railroad acquired the PWB in 1881. *From* Distinguished Railroad Men of America, *1890.*

Within a few months, the PRR was officially cutting the PWB's ties with Boston, for example informing Kidder, Peabody & Co. that most of its former services to the railroad would no longer be required. By May 1882, there was a formal agreement between the PWB and its Delaware Railroad, the Pennsy and its United Railroads of New Jersey and others for the exchange of traffic over the roads of their respective companies.

By taking control of the PWB, the Pennsy had gained 263 miles of PWB main line, plus 330 miles of branches, as well as additional terminals in both Philadelphia and Baltimore. Most contemporary accounts of the takeover failed to even mention that wither went the PWB so went the Delaware Railroad. So, though it might not have figured greatly, if at all, in the decision, the PWB deal also gave the Pennsy the Delaware Railroad's north–south main line and its growing feeder empire on the Delmarva Peninsula.

Over the following several years, it seemed that the Pennsy worked to bring the Delaware Railroad's feeder empire under direct control of its newly acquired PWB. The Queen Anne and Kent Railroad had been reorganized by the PWB in 1877, following a mortgage foreclosure sale, but it had operated as a separate entity until 1881, when PWB took over its operations. In 1882, the PWB acquired all the capital stock of the Maryland and Delaware Railroad, which had also undergone sale at foreclosure in 1877. In 1883, the Dorchester and Delaware Railroad was reorganized as the Cambridge and Seaford Railroad by the PWB. In 1885, the PWB became the operator of the newly formed Delaware, Maryland and Virginia Railroad Company.

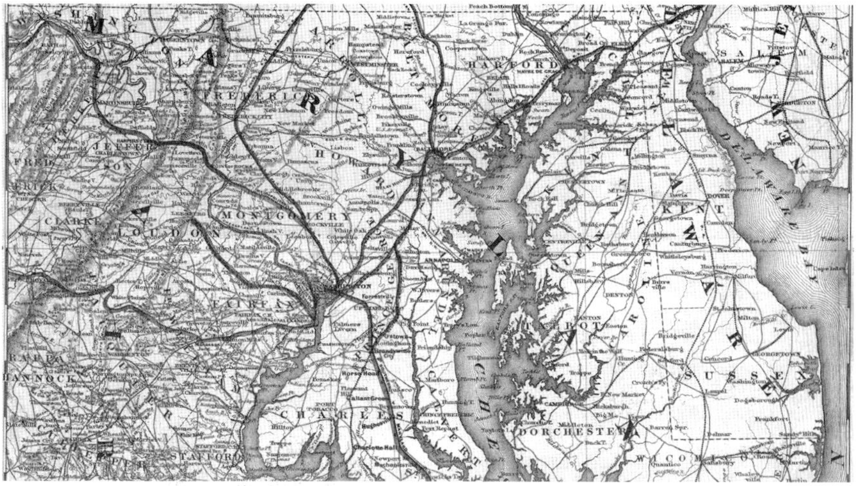

This 1881 map, drawn just before construction of the NYP&N, shows the route of the Delaware Railroad and the feeder system it spawned. *Library of Congress, Geography and Map Division.*

Yet the overall state of transportation on the Delmarva Peninsula in the mid-1880s remained relatively primitive. The tentacles of the Delaware Railroad's feeder empire consisted of lightly built single-track lines. Yes, one could get to Philadelphia, New York, Baltimore or Norfolk from the upper Delmarva Peninsula, but it could take over twenty hours to do so. The peninsula's connection with Norfolk had yet to become the nucleus of a north–south thoroughfare that earlier visionaries had imagined. And to get from one larger Eastern Shore town in Maryland to another, one had to travel from one feeder railroad to another via a journey through Delaware on the Delaware Railroad.

You can still find artifacts of these early days of railroading on the Eastern Shore. Late in January 2014, Mat and I decided to explore the remains of the New Castle and Frenchtown Rail Road on the Maryland side of the state line. They were not too hard to find, since the State of Maryland had placed part of the railroad's old route in the National Register. But first we went looking for old Frenchtown, which vintage maps suggested lay at the end of what is now called Frenchtown Road. We drove between fields, fallow at that time of year, passed a few modest houses and then entered a wooded area where the road was lined with houses on both sides. Then Frenchtown Road turned into a dirt road as it continued into the woods. Google satellite maps showed us the dirt road led into a bayside swamp where no structures remained, so we aborted that particular exploration and returned to Route 213, the modern-day successor to the old road south from Elkton.

We then turned east on Lewis Shore Road, where a historic marker confirmed that we had located the New Castle and Frenchtown Rail Road road bed. The road ran through a pretty copse, and we stopped and parked where another historic marker informed us we were about to cross the railroad's original bridge across a creek. Unfortunately, it was impossible to see the bridge beneath us from the road. I did locate what seemed to be a path leading down from the road through the woods to the creek, but it was steep and icy. Even when we returned a couple of months later and I was wearing flats, I found the path too steep for an easy descent, but I got close enough to get a view of the stone bridge through the trees, if not a decent photograph. We kept on driving, searching for any other remaining railroad artifacts, but the next sign we came across was one informing us we were about to enter private property. In the distance, we could see some nice-looking waterfront residences, presumably on the site of the railroad's old wharf, and beyond them the silvery surface of the Elk River.

The New Castle and Wilmington Railroad, or the eastern extension of the old New Castle and Frenchtown Rail Road built by the PWB, is still in operation. Norfolk Southern now uses it to bring trains from Wilmington on to the Delmarva Peninsula.

Trains are also still running on the old Kent County Rail Road, thanks to its modern-day successor, called the Maryland and Delaware Railroad, but only as far as Worton. The old railbed into Chestertown was converted to a rail trail after the modern Maryland and Delaware Railroad closed its riverside Chestertown rail yard.

Chestertown boasts a number of railroad artifacts among the attractions of this now somewhat touristy college town, but these have nothing to do with the early days of railroading. At the base of Chestertown's Cross Street, there's a passenger station built circa 1902–3, a time when the Kent County Rail Road had been liberated from its New Jersey connections to come under the control of the Pennsylvania Railroad. The building long served as the headquarters of the *Tidewater Trader*, a local weekly newspaper short on editorial and long on advertising, but in 2016, the *Tidewater Trader* moved its headquarters and put the building up for rent.

Between the station and the Chester River, in what was once the rail yard and river landing, there's a large timber building whose size and shape suggest a former grain mill. Called Stepne Station, it housed a couple of shops and a conference center in 2014. At its rear was a disconnected section of railroad

The New Castle and Frenchtown Rail Road arch lies beneath this road just under the guard rail. *Author's collection.*

The passenger station in Chestertown, Maryland, built after PRR had taken control of the Kent County Railroad. *Author's collection.*

track left in place to support a caboose and two passenger cars, for which we found no obvious explanation. No signage identified the railroad they came from or what purpose they then served. The Chestertown town manager explained that they belonged to the owner of Stepne Station, who brought them in simply because he liked the way they looked on the property.

Easton has a vintage railroad station that long served as the town's visitor center. It was housing an organization called the Chesapeake Wildlife Heritage Organization when we stopped in during the spring of 2014. The young folks working the desks inside didn't know anything about the railroad station, but they had a brochure titled *Rails through Easton* ready to hand us, so obviously, we were not the first to inquire. The brochure described the construction of the Delaware Railroad, the original Maryland and Delaware Railroad and the Baltimore, Chesapeake & Atlantic Railroad, which also once served Easton, but it maddeningly failed to mention just which railroad Easton's repurposed railroad station had belonged to.

For the record, it was the passenger station of the original Maryland and Delaware Railroad. I found a map of Easton drawn in 1877, not long after the completion of the Maryland and Delaware Railroad. It clearly depicted the railroad's depots and the engine and freight houses of its small rail yard, which also had a limited turntable. The passenger depot stood at the corner of Railroad Avenue and West Avenue, the exact location of Easton's now-repurposed railroad station. Railroad Avenue has since been renamed Goldsborough Street after a prominent citizen, and West Avenue has been renamed Pennsylvania Avenue after the prominent railroad that would eventually dominate the Eastern Shore. Outside the station, there's a rail trail named Easton Rails to Trails, constructed on a two-and-a-half-mile segment of the original Maryland and Delaware Railroad.

In tiny Sudlersville, there's a small train station that once served the Queen Anne and Kent Railroad. It is not that town's original depot but rather the "new" station, built in 1885. Purchased in 1987 by the Sudlersville Community Betterment Club, it is maintained as a museum of railroad and town history and is occasionally opened to the public. Similarly, the train station in Georgetown, Delaware, once served the Junction and Breakwater Railroad, but it was constructed in 1892, not during the 1850s, when the line opened, or during its 1870s extension. It was purchased by the Historic Georgetown Association in 1996, and it is occasionally open for special events.

The jewel of the Eastern Shore's early railroading days, the Delaware Railroad, is now part of the Delmarva Central Railroad, a subsidiary of

This field was once the terminus of the Kent County Railroad. The railroad cars belong to the current property owner. *Author's collection.*

This structure was once the passenger station for the Maryland and Delaware Railroad in Easton, Maryland. *Author's collection.*

Carload Express, a short line that operates a total of 188 miles of railroad in Delaware, Maryland and Virginia. The Delmarva Central hauls freight, including food, lumber, liquid chemicals and coal, but operates no passenger trains. There are a number of back roads in Delaware with vantage points where you can occasionally see a freight or coal train parked or in operation.

You will find vintage passenger stations along the route of the original Delaware Railroad in towns like Clayton, Harrington and Dover, either standing vacant or having been repurposed. However, these were all constructed by the Pennsylvania Railroad, following its acquisition of the Philadelphia, Wilmington and Baltimore Railroad.

The Delmarva Central Railroad has trackage rights over the eastern half of what was once the New Castle and Frenchtown Rail Road between New Castle and the town of Porter, which was the original northern terminus of the Delaware Railroad.

In the town of New Castle, Delaware, there's a tiny wood frame building in a public park on the Delaware River that is purported to have been the ticket office of the New Castle and Frenchtown Rail Road. There's been some controversy over the age of this building and the purpose it originally served, but if it was indeed built in 1832, like the sign on the side of the building would have one believe, it would be one of the earliest railroading artifacts on the Delmarva Peninsula.

The old Chesapeake and Delaware Canal has also managed to survive. Unlike many other early canals, it was not quickly rendered obsolete by increasingly efficient railroad technology, because for a considerable time, it remained easier to ship freight this way from the Delaware River to the Chesapeake Bay. Where the old road south from Elkton, now Route 213, crosses the canal, you can visit Chesapeake City, which grew from a single tavern and canal tollhouse into a thriving town that became home to many people who earned their living maintaining the canal and facilitating transportation through it. The locals officially adopted the name Chesapeake City in 1839. Today, it's a popular tourist destination, where some of its nineteenth-century structures now house bed-and-breakfasts and gift shops. It also has a number of restaurants overlooking the canal, where one is likely to see a passing barge being conducted by a tugboat. When cabin fever hits us in the winter, we drive down for crab cakes and a water view.

In Virginia, you won't find similar artifacts of the early era of internal improvements, because prior to the 1880s, folks on Virginia's eastern shore were still living in the eighteenth century. The fastest way to travel remained by steamboat or schooner from one port to another. Overland public transportation was limited to a stage line that carried the U.S. mail and passengers between Horntown in Accomack County to Eastville in Northampton County. In his 1879 article for *Harper's New Monthly Magazine*, Howard Pyle described waiting for the stage at 4:00 a.m., when "a curious spectacle came limping and hobbling along, with many eccentric lurchings and side movements—a white horse with a preposterously deformed leg, harnessed to a crazy wagon, creeping through the shadows of the pine glades." Pyle asked the driver if he had seen the stage, and the man replied, "Wa'al, I reckon this yers the stage," adding that his horse was "jest as good a hoss as you'll find in Northampton County."

The stage stopped at Bell Haven, where Pyle ate breakfast in "a queer little tavern," and when he went to get back on the stage, he discovered "the late dilapidated white animal replaced by a vicious-looking black, with a straight neck, a backbone that sagged in the middle, and sharp little promontories at the points of his shoulders and hips." Pyle concluded, "Certainly, considering how the mail-carrier of Northampton endangers life and limb, not to speak of patience, he deserves the palm for patriotic disinterestedness and self-sacrifice."

3

The Pennsy and Its People Look South Toward the Eastern Shore

When the Pennsylvania Railroad Company was chartered in April 1846, its acknowledged purpose was to facilitate transportation between eastern and western Pennsylvania, especially to and from the emerging metropolis of Pittsburgh. Its charter appeared to assume there would be no need for it to do business beyond the commonwealth's boundaries. But that charter did not prevent other railroads from being chartered and built in Pennsylvania to tap the commonwealth's natural resources and bring them to market, nor did it prohibit railroads chartered in other states from attempting to do business in Pennsylvania. Those in control of the B&O Railroad had always intended to extend tracks into Pittsburgh, but the same year the Pennsy was chartered, another bill was passed rescinding B&O's permission to enter the commonwealth if the Pennsy managed to win a race against time with certain construction and financing goals. From the earliest years of its history, the Pennsy was no stranger to vicious competition, and early on, the railroad developed a program fostering expansion beyond the limitations of its charter, mainly through acquisitions, like its takeover of the Philadelphia, Wilmington and Baltimore Railroad.

In 1846, Pennsylvania already had a trans-commonwealth transportation system commonly called the Main Line of Public Works. Constructed at public expense, it incorporated a railroad from Philadelphia to the town of Columbia on the eastern shore of the Susquehanna River. West of the river, freight and passengers had to be moved from a canal to a mountain portage railroad and then to another canal that brought traffic into downtown

Pittsburgh. The system had been in operation since the 1830s, but the need to transfer freight and passengers from one kind of vehicle to another made transportation difficult and slow.

By the 1840s, the merchants of Philadelphia were agitating for a continuous railroad linking Philadelphia and Pittsburgh, and the Pennsy's initial mission was to replace the canal-rail-canal system west of the Susquehanna with a railroad linking Harrisburg and Pittsburgh. By 1849, the Pennsy was running trains between Harrisburg and Lewisburg. By 1850, the PRR had constructed tracks east from Pittsburgh to Turtle Creek. By the end of 1852, the Pennsy was able to get its first train all the way to Pittsburgh without shifting freight or passengers into canal boats.

However, cars carrying freight and passengers still had to be hauled over the Allegheny Ridge by the state-owned Allegheny Portage Railroad. In two more years, the PRR mountain division made the old portage railroad obsolete with the construction of its magnificent Horseshoe Curve, a modified switchback system that lengthened the route but reduced the grade over the steep ridge that separated the eastern part of the commonwealth from the Allegheny Plateau.

The PRR's 1846 charter allowed the railroad to construct only a single branch from Pittsburgh to Erie but gave permission for the Pennsy to build smaller feeder branches into any county through which its main line passed. Had PRR management adhered strictly to these terms, the Pennsy would never have earned the nickname Standard Railroad of the World. The Pennsy made its first acquisition as early as 1848, when PRR leased the Harrisburg, Portsmouth, Mount Joy & Lancaster Rail-road. In 1855, the Pennsy just about doubled its physical plant by offering Pennsylvania's secretary of state $7.5 million for the Philadelphia & Columbia Railroad, which had been constructed as one component of the commonwealth's Main Line of Public Works. The sale was completed at the Philadelphia Merchants' Exchange in 1857.

Although the Civil War made tremendous demands on many northern railroads, including the Pennsy, for new tracks and rolling stock, the company continued to grow by securing control of the Cumberland Valley Railroad, the Northern Central Railway and the Philadelphia and Erie Railroad, making it the dominant railroad in the state of Pennsylvania and a corporation that was already gaining skill in empire building.

In the wake of the Civil War, the Pennsy greatly extended its reach both east and west. By the end of the 1860s, PRR leased the Pittsburgh, Fort Wayne & Chicago Railway, giving it lines reaching northwest to Chicago. PRR also leased a collection of smaller rail operations known as the Panhandle Lines connecting Pittsburgh with Cincinnati and St. Louis, as well as Chicago. To offer transportation to East Coast cities other than Philadelphia, in 1871, PRR leased the United Railroad Companies of New Jersey, giving it a route through Jersey to the Hudson River and access via ferry to New York City.

Extending PRR service to the nation's capital was a next logical step. Through its control of the Northern Central Railway, PRR had its own route into Baltimore since 1861. However, the B&O Railroad, the Pennsy's rival since the very day PRR was chartered, had the only rail line from the north and east into Washington, D.C. Known as the B&O's Washington Branch Railroad, the route was a state-sanctioned monopoly for which the B&O paid the State of Maryland a fee for each passenger carried. Passengers riding the Pennsy to Baltimore could get to D.C. via the B&O, but the B&O seemed to go out of its way to complicate this process. The B&O refused to cooperate with the Pennsy by offering through ticketing or baggage handling or even establishing schedules that facilitated changing trains.

The B&O seemed equally loath to cooperate with the planters of southern Maryland by constructing a branch from Baltimore to the Potomac River south of D.C. Members of the prominent Bowie family had been agitating for such rail service since the 1850s, resulting in Maryland's legislature granting a charter for the Baltimore and Potomac Rail Road Company in 1853. Surveys were begun in 1859, and after the Civil War was over, Oden Bowie approached both John W. Garrett of the B&O and Tom Scott of the Pennsy for help in getting construction started. Garrett turned him down, but Scott was interested.

That was because the yet-unbuilt railroad's charter had an interesting provision. Besides authorizing a main line from Baltimore to an old tobacco port called Pope's Creek on the lower Potomac, the Baltimore and Potomac was permitted to construct lateral branches up to twenty miles in length from any point on its main line. That was just far enough to make it possible for the Baltimore and Potomac to have a branch running into Washington, D.C.

In 1866, a man named George Washington Cass entered in a contract with other investors to finance and construct the Baltimore and Potomac Rail Road. Cass is known primarily as the president of the Northern Pacific Railway, but at that time, he was president of the Pittsburgh, Fort Wayne & Chicago Railway, a position he had held since 1857 and would continue to hold until 1883, well after this railroad was leased to the PRR in 1869. In 1867, after Pennsylvania's U.S. senator Simon Cameron ushered a bill through

Congress allowing the Baltimore and Potomac to extend a lateral branch into the District of Columbia, PRR directors finally accepted Cass's proposition and authorized $400,000 to construct the Baltimore and Potomac. In 1868, it was actually the Pennsy that commenced the new railroad's construction. When Oden Bowie took office as governor of Maryland in 1869, PRR had a powerful ally in position to oppose any Maryland bill that might have stymied construction. The Baltimore and Potomac's "branch" to D.C. was finished in 1872, while its "main line" to Pope's Creek, which would always be very lightly used, didn't open until 1873.

A couple of tunnels and a bridge gave PRR an efficient and convenient all-rail route from Philadelphia to Washington, D.C. In 1873, a Baltimore and Potomac tunnel connected that railroad to the Pennsy's Northern Central Railway. A second tunnel extended it to the PWB. In 1870, Congress authorized the Baltimore and Potomac to extend its D.C. branch to the "Long Bridge" over the Potomac, providing the railroad maintained it and allowed other railroads to use it. This took the exclusive use of this bridge away from the B&O and, incidentally, gave PRR a connection to Virginia's railroads. Thanks to both Congress and municipal officials in the District of Columbia, the D.C. station of the Baltimore and Potomac Rail Road was centrally located, making it convenient for travelers to the nation's capital.

Gaining access to Washington, D.C., over PRR-controlled tracks might have been an initial step in a bigger PRR plan to expand throughout the postwar South, offering service to cities as distant as New Orleans and Atlanta by means of the then well-established PRR expansion model of acquiring other railroads. Most antebellum southern railroads connected the hinterlands with port cities, such as Charleston and Savannah. The Pennsy's management team was not alone in thinking it was high time to connect the larger cities of the South with one another by means of air lines, or routes constructed more or less on the most efficient, if not the shortest, distance between two points, thus creating a more integrated network rail system throughout the South.

While construction of the Baltimore and Potomac was just getting started, the Pennsy demonstrated its interest in southern railroad expansion and its willingness to invest in this cause. In 1868, Tom Scott and J. Donald Cameron, Simon Cameron's son, attended a meeting in Baltimore convened by two Baltimore bankers, William Thompson Walters and Benjamin Franklin Newcomer, who were heavily invested in two North Carolina railroads and interested in purchasing another. At a subsequent meeting in 1870, Scott mentioned that PRR would be needing traffic for its Baltimore and Potomac subsidiary and his belief that southern railroads could provide it if they were well-capitalized and integrated.

In 1871, PRR sponsored the creation of the Southern Railway Security Company (SRSC), a holding company intended to gain control through stock ownership of southern railroads that could be used to create through lines between major northern and southern cities. According to the Pennsylvania Railroad company's 1871 annual report, the Pennsy became a major SRSC investor "to protect its investment in the Baltimore and Potomac Railroad." Its model might have been PRR's Pennsylvania Company, a holding company chartered in 1870 to take charge of PRR's system west of Pittsburgh.

The men controlling and managing the SRSC holding company included a number of PRR executives, most notably John Edgar Thomson and Thomas A. Scott. Others included some who had attended the 1868 and 1870 meetings, including Baltimore bankers Walters and Newcomer and J. Donald Cameron. PRR ally George Washington Cass was president of the SRSC, but Scott was probably the company's real director behind the scenes. Southerners even referred to the SRSC as the "Tom Scott."

During the following two years, the SRSC went railroad shopping and managed to pick up thirteen railroads, uniting them into several trunk lines extending from Richmond: along the Atlantic coast, inland to Atlanta and westward to the Mississippi. For relatively few bucks, the PRR had essentially gained control of over two thousand miles of southern tracks.

This accomplishment had been achieved despite considerable opposition. Tom Scott was a northerner, a capitalist and had served as assistant secretary of war during the Civil War, in control of the Union's railroads and telegraph lines. To many southerners, Scott was an outsider, a money-grubbing carpetbagger and a Yankee who had played a key role in ending their way of life and dreams of independence. In an article titled "Swindling the South," published in the *Richmond Whig* and reprinted in the *Macon Weekly Telegraph* in February 1872, the author characterized the SRSC's acquisitions as hostile takeovers whose perpetrators would readily sacrifice the interests of private minority shareholders for their own gain, commenting, "This is the game of these adventurers for swindling, on a gigantic scale, the widows and orphans of the South." The author was no doubt equating SRSC with other carpetbagging railroad rings organized in the late 1860s whose leaders had pocketed considerable money from bond issues.

The SRSC eventually succumbed not to southern resentment but to the depression caused by the financial Panic of 1873, which created losses and bankruptcies for many railroads. The Pennsy was in no danger of bankruptcy, but by 1873, it was becoming clear that the profits it had anticipated from southern traffic were being extremely slow to materialize. The Pennsy made a retrenchment decision to withdraw from the SRSC and limit its own growth to the territory that PRR had historically dominated: north of the Ohio and Potomac Rivers and east of the Mississippi. The SRSC did serve as a model for future successful consolidations and railroad expansion in the South. It also gave the Pennsy the bonus of blocking any southern expansion plans for its archrival the B&O.

Back when PRR executive management was formally organized in 1847, the company was run by a board of thirteen members under the leadership of Samuel V. Merrick, a prominent Philadelphia manufacturer. For its original chief engineer, the Pennsy hired J. Edgar Thomson, who had made the surveys for the state-run Philadelphia & Columbia Railroad. The board elected Thomson president in 1852, and he held the position until his death in 1874. By the 1870s, the PRR had an organization chart that reflected its growth during the previous twenty years. The president was assisted by four vice presidents, their own assistants and a corporate secretary. The company was divided into geographical divisions and corporate departments.

The Pennsy had become a place where an able and talented man could rise through the ranks. Historians have commented on the "symbiotic partnership" of Thomson and Thomas A. Scott, who had joined the PRR as a station agent in 1850, moving up to general superintendent in 1858 and first vice president in 1860. Scott balanced Thomson's engineering expertise with his own charisma, daring and political savvy. The two men agreed completely on the importance of the Pennsy's financial success, and together, they presided over a period of fiscally responsible growth and expansion, earning much investor confidence. Scott became president in 1874. He found a protégé very much in his own image in Alexander Johnston Cassatt.

For a business titan whose name at the time of his death was as recognizable as that of the president of the United States, it is puzzling that Cassatt has inspired only a single biography. It was published in 1978 by Neale Watson Academic Publications, and its depressing title was *End of the Line: Alexander J. Cassatt and the Pennsylvania Railroad*. Its author was not an academic but rather a former newspaper reporter who had studied American history at Bryn Mawr College and received a master's degree in 1967. Prior to *End of the Line*, Patricia Talbot Davis had written two books on Philadelphia-area history, both published by small houses: one about the construction of Beth Sholom Synagogue in Elkins Park and the other a history of the Curwen family.

In a 1980 article published by a township historical society, Davis described the serendipitous discovery that prompted her to write about Cassatt. She wrote, "James Dallett, archivist at the University of Pennsylvania, pleasantly impressed by my work, introduced me to the late Mrs. John B. Thayer [Cassatt's granddaughter Lois], who had in her possession a collection of family letters, several thousand of them. She thought there might be a book in them. Would I read them and see?" Davis reported that she was warned by historians and publishers not to attempt a Cassatt biography. At that time, the Pennsy's business records were not open to researchers, but Mrs. Thayer encouraged her and gave her sole and unrestricted access to the Cassatt family letters.

The resulting biography got tepid reviews. Those reviewing it for scholarly journals accepted it as a decent reflection of the lifestyles of nineteenth-century folk who could afford European vacations and country estates. However, they noted that it contained significant errors of fact. Albro Martin of Harvard University, reviewing *End of the Line* for the *Journal of American History*, was particularly harsh, arguing that Davis lacked the background in business and railroad history to put Cassatt in the proper context, writing, "While she longs to rescue Cassatt from the 'robber baron' mire, her inability to rise above the conventional ignorance is fatal." The scholarly reviewers were also steamed that the book had no footnotes and no sufficiently detailed bibliography.

For whatever reason, following publication of *End of the Line* and the death of Mrs. Thayer, her heirs made the family letters unavailable to other scholars. The records of the Pennsylvania Railroad Company, on the other hand, were organized and cataloged by Hagley Museum and Library, the Pennsylvania State Archives and Temple University, among other institutions. When I began researching this book in 2013, I was convinced that by that time the Cassatt descendants must have donated such a significant collection of letters to some repository where they'd be available to researchers. I proceeded to contact the Academy of Natural Sciences, the American Philosophical Society, the Historical Society of Pennsylvania, Winterthur Museum and Library, the Lower Merion Historical Society, the Chester County Historical Society and the special collections departments at Drexel University, Franklin and Marshall College, the University of Pennsylvania, LaSalle University, Lehigh University, the University of Delaware and Rensselaer Polytechnic Institute (Cassatt's alma mater). Everybody told me that the papers had not arrived at their institution, but the director of libraries at LaSalle wrote that a staff member had discovered in the description of the Mary Cassatt materials at the Smithsonian a note saying that a collection of Cassatt family letters had been donated to the Philadelphia Museum of Art.

In a way, it made sense. Alexander Cassatt used to be the most famous member of this family, but sometime during the twentieth century, the reputation of his artist sister, Mary, eclipsed his own. I contacted the art museum, and its archivist sent me a cordial invitation to visit and an inventory of 175 letters penned by various members of the Cassatt family to one another dating from the late 1870s to the 1890s. This collection did not sound like the "several thousand" letters that Davis had described, but most of the letters housed at the art museum had been written during the very period of Alexander Cassatt's life that I was most interested in: the years when the New York, Philadelphia, and Norfolk Railroad was being organized, constructed and opened for business.

I'll take the word of Ms. Davis for the story of the early life of Alexander Johnston Cassatt, whom she tells us was known to his family as Aleck. Cassatt was born on December 8, 1839, in Pittsburgh. During his early childhood, his family moved to a nearby mill town then called Allegheny City, where his father, Robert Cassatt, established himself as a manufacturer and banker. While Aleck was still a child, the family moved to a town called Hardwicke and then to Philadelphia, where Robert Cassatt established the banking firm of Lloyd, Cassatt & Company.

When his father retired, Aleck moved with his family to Paris and then Heidelberg, where he attended boarding school. When the rest of the Cassatt family returned to the United States in 1855, Alexander Cassatt remained behind at Darmstadt University of Technology, where he studied engineering. On his own return to the United States, Cassatt enrolled at Yale but left that prestigious school to enter Rensselaer Polytechnic Institute in Troy, New York, graduating in 1859 with a degree in civil engineering. His first job was rodman, or surveyor, for a railroad in Georgia.

When Cassatt became president of the Pennsylvania Railroad Company in 1899, the office of the railroad's secretary published a biographical pamphlet that described his career at the Pennsy, where he came to work in 1861. Cassatt started as a rodman in its Philadelphia Division and then joined the railroad's engineer corps in the construction of the railway linking the PRR line with the Philadelphia and Trenton Railroad. In 1864, Cassatt was promoted to resident engineer of the railroad's Middle Division. In 1866, he became superintendent of Motive Power and Machinery of the PRR subsidiary called the Philadelphia and Erie Railroad, and then in 1867, he became superintendent of Motive Power and Machinery for the entire PRR. In 1870, Cassatt became general superintendent of the Pennsylvania Railroad. After the Pennsy leased the United Railroads of New Jersey in 1871, Cassatt was promoted to general manager of Lines East of Pittsburgh and Erie. After Thomson died and Scott became PRR president, Cassatt was promoted to third vice president. He became first vice president after Scott retired in 1880.

If there was any blemish on Cassatt's sterling PRR record, Cassatt likely earned it during the summer of 1877, when he was among the few PRR executives on hand to receive the disturbing news of labor unrest in Pittsburgh. Thanks to the depression that followed the financial Panic of 1873, PRR had cut its workers' wages and instituted new work rules, which cut costs for the railroad but further decreased the workers' incomes. Cassatt traveled to Pittsburgh and made what turned out to be a serious error of judgment when he asked the Philadelphia Militia, which had been brought in to restore order, to clear the PRR tracks of protesting strikers who were preventing the railroad from moving its trains. The resulting riot claimed the lives of a number of demonstrators and destroyed much of the railroad's facilities in Pittsburgh. Reporters covering the event, as well as many Pittsburgh residents and later many labor historians, tended to blame Cassatt for the entire debacle.

Cassatt certainly had the respect of contemporaries who wrote about him. In an 1886 article appearing in the *Juniata Sentinel and Republican* titled "Couldn't Scare A.J. Cassatt," an engineer named Jim Sanford told a story about the time Cassatt had joined him in the locomotive of an express train from Jersey City to Philadelphia. To see whether he could get a rise out of the suited executive, Sanford accelerated to seventy-seven miles per hour. Sanford was quoted as saying, "I was a leetle scairt myself, not bein' sartin if the machine would hang together at that frightful pace." But Cassatt just turned to him and calmly inquired, "Can't she go any faster than this?"

Francis Barksdale also mentioned that Cassatt got on well with PRR employees in his 1901 article for the *World's Work* in which he reported on Cassatt's role in the acquisition of PWB. Barksdale wrote, "While Mr. Cassatt was firm and determined in his relations with the army of men under his control, he was not dictatorial nor severe, and no official ever enjoyed in higher degree the confidence and respect of his subordinates."

Barksdale also described Cassatt as bold and intelligent but a man of few words. This opinion was shared by the author of Cassatt's obituary in the *Railroad Gazette*, who wrote, "Mr. Cassatt was a diffident man, painfully shy before an audience of any size, but at a directors' meeting or in conferences with his officers, speaking quickly to the point and as incisively as he thought."

An un-bylined profile of Cassatt reprinted from the *New York Evening Post* and appearing in the July 8, 1906 issue of *Railroad Gazette* also described Cassatt as "one of the most diffident of men" but one who was very comfortable with the lifestyle that his wealth made possible. It described his office at PRR's Philadelphia headquarters as a large room "guarded by four Negro porters and flanked round by one secretary, three stenographers and three officials who have the title of 'assistant to the [PRR] president.'" Having been a "gay, rollicking blade in his youthful days," he lived "in regal fashion" at his mansion in Haverford but liked to entertain distinguished guests less formally at his farm in Chesterbrook. He belonged to the New York Yacht Club and "has ridden horseback so much that his legs are quite bowed."

Several contemporaries described Cassatt as insightful and forward thinking. Barksdale noted that Cassatt had been the first prominent railroad executive to recognize the value of air brakes. After Cassatt died in 1906, his *Railroad Gazette* obituary and a memorial tribute in the PRR board minutes both credited Cassatt with recognizing early in his term as PRR president that the railroad would need to expand to meet the needs of America's growing industries. As PRR president, Cassatt invested in the securities of the B&O, the Norfolk and Western, the Chesapeake and Ohio Railroads and secured a controlling interest in the Long Island Railroad. His greatest achievements had yet to be completed at the time of his death, namely, the tunnels beneath the Hudson River that would bring Pennsy trains to a magnificent station in Manhattan.

In a 1905 book titled *The Strategy of Great Railroads*, author Frank Spearman noted that Cassatt was not without critics. Some folks thought he moved too far too fast, that he was "reckless of the interests of investors, the opinion of the public, and the common rights of property." But criticism from Cassatt's contemporaries is pretty hard to find. In their memorial tribute, the PRR directors concluded, "All those brought into contact with him, recognized in him one of the leading spirits of our age, one of the men who make a nation great, and one whose fame is a precious heritage for his country."

For a man so ambitious and perceptive who had obtained the position of first vice president of the Pennsylvania Railroad Company at the youthful age of forty-one, it seems strange that he abruptly retired from the company at the age of forty-two. It's been suggested that Cassatt did not get along with George B. Roberts, who had been acting as PRR president since Tom Scott left for a lengthy trip to improve his health following a series of strokes in

Left: Alexander Cassatt, president of the NYP&N from 1885 to 1899. *Library of Congress.*

Below: The tower at Pocomoke City, Maryland, named for Alexander Cassatt. *Cape Charles Historical Society, Photograph Collection.*

1878. Yet Cassatt and Roberts had worked together without conflict for some time, most significantly on the PWB acquisition. It's also been suggested that by selecting Roberts, not Cassatt, to succeed Scott following Scott's formal resignation in June 1880, the PRR directors were signaling a move toward a more conservative and less expansionist policy that would not have suited Cassatt. Cassatt's resignation followed rumors that he was leaving to become president of another railroad, but Cassatt's letter of resignation sated that his primary motive was simply a desire for more leisure time.

Although Cassatt took his family to Europe about six weeks later, he retained an office in Philadelphia, and in September 1883, he was elected to the PRR board. According to Barksdale, "There was no important meeting of the board at which he failed to appear, unless absence from the country prevented his attendance."

When Roberts presented Cassatt's letter of resignation at the PRR board meeting held on September 13, 1882, he told the directors that Cassatt had assured him "should he determine at any future time to reenter the railroad service he would make the PRR his first consideration." The board accepted Cassatt's resignation, noting in their minutes that they took pleasure "in the assurance that in the future as in the past everything tending to promote the welfare and prosperity of this Company will receive his earnest and cordial support."

It makes one wonder. Did Cassatt really leave the Pennsy? Or was his resignation just a formality allowing him to work for the PRR in another capacity while they collaborated on yet another expansion and acquisition plan, one that would smoothly extend the Pennsy's reach into the South and finally bring to bear the rail-water link between Philadelphia and Norfolk that had been envisioned by many since the early days of railroading? After all, the Pennsy's 1881 acquisition of the PWB, and therefore the Delaware Railroad, had already rather abruptly given the Pennsy tracks extending about halfway down the Delmarva Peninsula.

4

The NYP&N: A New Line to Norfolk

In the 1850s, while the Philadelphia, Wilmington and Baltimore Railroad was financing the Delaware Railroad, Virginians persisted in trying to get a north–south line constructed on their portion of the Eastern Shore. In 1853, Virginia issued a charter for the North and South Railroad Company. In 1855, the general assembly followed up with a charter for an interstate railroad called the Norfolk Air Line Railroad, linking Snow Hill in Maryland with Eastville, the seat of Virginia's Northampton County. Neither of these projects got past the planning and surveying stages.

Meanwhile, Maryland promoters revived the 1833 Eastern Shore Railroad Company (ESRR) in 1853. Its proposed southern terminus would remain a port on Tangier Sound that would hopefully yet become a gateway to Norfolk, but its new northern terminus would be the southern end of the line of the Delaware Railroad, then still under construction, not Elkton as originally planned.

An 1874 note in the board meeting minutes of the Eastern Shore Railroad refers to a contract made in 1859 between the Philadelphia, Wilmington and Baltimore Railroad and the new Eastern Shore Railroad, stating that PWB would operate this railroad and cooperate in making it a success. In March 1859, the *Baltimore Sun* described the new Eastern Shore as an "extension of the Delaware Railroad."

The Delaware Railroad planned to build the thirteen miles of ESRR track in Delaware, while ESRR promoters in Maryland lobbied the state for the balance of the $1 million subsidy that had been allocated for internal

John W. Crisfield, a Maryland congressman and president of the Eastern Shore Railroad Company. *Library of Congress.*

improvements on the Eastern Shore over twenty years earlier. In 1858, citizens gathered for mass meetings in Snow Hill and Salisbury. In March 1859, the Eastern Shore Appropriations Bill passed Maryland's senate and house, and the ESRR was assured of a significant share of the $1 million.

ESRR commissioners had already been receiving private stock subscriptions, and its stockholders met in the town of Princess Anne in February 1859 to elect directors who organized a board with John W.

Crisfield as president. A Delaware Railroad engineer had already surveyed a route from Delmar via Salisbury to a spot on Tangier Sound, then called Annamessix, and by March 26, 1859, the *Easton Gazette* reported, "Next Tuesday the work will be opened on the ground."

A significant factor in the long delay of the commencement of ESRR construction was certainly the strong opposition of the merchants of the Chesapeake's Western Shore. By the 1850s, the pages of local Eastern Shore newspapers were full of advertisements placed by the operators of schooners and steamboats that offered to deliver passengers and freight from smaller Eastern Shore ports like Cambridge, Oxford, St. Michaels, Denton and Easton to the wharves of Baltimore. Freight that would be able to travel between these towns and Norfolk or Philadelphia via emerging feeders, a new Eastern Shore Railroad and the Delaware Railroad would be business that bypassed Baltimore completely. In April 1857, the *Baltimore Republican* printed an editorial stating, "No true friend of the State would advocate the construction of a road whose only chance of success depends upon the diversion of trade and travel from their own commercial metropolis [meaning Baltimore]. Such a suicidal policy could not be pursued by any patriot even if his own little pecuniary interest should be temporarily benefitted thereby." The editors of the *Easton Gazette* tersely replied that ships could sail just as easily between Tangier Sound and Baltimore as they could travel to Norfolk. Furthermore, should the Eastern Shore Railroad project die, Virginia had some already chartered railroads whose construction would divert trade and travel farther south and still farther from Baltimore.

Unlike the merchants of Baltimore, the business community of Philadelphia favored the fledgling ESRR while it was under construction. In October 1860, Philadelphia's Board of Trade sent a committee to Princess Anne, where they met with the ESRR board of directors and the presidents of the Delaware Railroad and the Philadelphia, Wilmington and Baltimore Railroad. The *Sun* reported on October 12, "We learn that they seemed to be thoroughly impressed with the importance of the work to Philadelphia, and expressed themselves decidedly in favor of its final completion, pledging themselves to use whatever influence they possessed to obtain the aid necessary to its consummation."

ESRR construction was completed as far as Salisbury when the Civil War officially started in 1861. While the war effort delayed further construction, the existence of rail service turned sleepy Salisbury into a Union garrison where Federal troops were stationed to quell any secessionist uprisings on the Delmarva Peninsula. In 1862, Virginia's Eastern Shore counties became part of the geographically distant Union state of West Virginia. West Virginia then incorporated the Accomack and Northampton Air Line Railroad Company to build a line between a ferry at Cherry Stone in Northampton County to the Maryland state line near Salisbury. John W. Crisfield of the ESRR was reported to favor the project.

It was not until 1865, when the Civil War was over, that the ESRR board ratified a contract to continue construction of the road from Salisbury to Somers Cove off of Tangier Sound. On June 23, the *Sun* reported that construction would "commence forthwith." In March 1866, the *Sun* announced that the ESRR had been formally opened to Princess Anne and that "two trains are running daily and regularly." In June 1866, Philadelphia's *North American* reported that ESRR trains would soon reach Somers Cove, where wharves were under construction and steamers were "in readiness" to connect the road to Norfolk. By November 1866, ESRR tracks had reached Somers Cove, which was renamed Crisfield in honor of the railroad's president.

Unfortunately, the Civil War had left the South's economy in ruins, and there was little need for steamboat traffic between Crisfield and Norfolk in the immediate postwar period. In the spring of 1867, ESRR expenses

The tracks of the Eastern Shore Railroad ran through the center of Crisfield, Maryland. *Cape Charles Historical Society, Photograph Collection.*

were considerably higher than receipts. In 1869, ESRR bondholders called for a reorganization to liquidate the railroad's debt to the PWB but to keep it running independent of the PWB since the potential for profit was certainly still there.

While business with Norfolk was slow to materialize, the ESRR became the catalyst in developing Crisfield as a different kind of commercial capital. In December 1868, the *Sun* reported, "Eleven car loads of oysters, in shell, were shipped from Crisfield to Philadelphia on Saturday. They averaged about 250 bushels to the car, making in all about 2,750 bushels. In addition to these, four of five tons of opened oysters were shipped." It turned out that Crisfield had been located conveniently near some of the Chesapeake Bay's best oystering waters. Within a few more years, Crisfield had become the central receiving depot for the bay's oystermen who brought the town and the Eastern Shore Railroad plenty of business that did not depend on a connection with Norfolk. In November 1871, the *Sun* explained, "The oysters are caught in the morning, opened in the course of the day, and shipped next morning to nearly every market on the continent, principally, however, to Pittsburgh, Pa., Troy, N.Y., and Buffalo. The town has increased in population some four hundred per cent within twelve months and if the packing houses are as successful this season as last it [Crisfield] will soon be incorporated."

The following year, Crisfield became the subject of a *New York Herald* story when an English steamer named the *Salsette* left the port with eighteen thousand bushels of oysters. The Fishmongers' Company of London had made the deal to replenish England's exhausted oyster beds with some of the Chesapeake's finest.

By the fall of 1872, a wharf 415 feet long that would support railroad tracks was nearly completed in Crisfield. The wharf was also designed to accommodate vessels carrying one hundred tons of cargo. The *Sun* published an anonymous letter from Crisfield documenting the town's remarkable growth from a place where "but one house stood upon the present site" to a boom town with twenty-nine to thirty oyster packinghouses and fifteen to twenty general merchandise stores doing $500,000 worth of business yearly. The letter also mentioned that the long-awaited regular and by then commercially viable water link to Norfolk had finally materialized: "Tri-weekly access to the South is furnished by the Clyde line of steamers to Norfolk."

The Eastern Shore Railroad finally began living up to its potential around the early 1870s. According to a statement of its treasurer in 1871, business was increasing each month. In addition to oysters, the railroad now also

Many oystering vessels landed cargo at Crisfield to be shipped by the Eastern Shore Railroad. *Cape Charles Historical Society, Photograph Collection.*

hauled produce and lumber, which was shipped from points along the railroad through Crisfield by water to New York. Boats also moved freight from the railroad's Crisfield terminus to Baltimore, as well as the ports of Virginia's Eastern Shore counties, in addition to its then daily service to Norfolk. However, throughout the 1870s, the ESRR remained in debt. In April 1878, the railroad's bondholders met in Philadelphia to agree on a plan to sell the railroad.

The timing of this proposed reorganization generally coincides with the creation of the Peninsula Railroad Company of Virginia, which occurred in March 1878. This new railroad was intended to run from the Virginia-

Maryland border down the length of Virginia's Eastern Shore to "any point on or near the Chesapeake Bay or Atlantic Ocean." It incorporated all Virginia's earlier chartered north–south railroads that were still waiting to be built. But to be a potentially profitable business proposition, the railroad would need to connect with Delmar—or at least with the tracks of the Eastern Shore Railroad.

Part of this gap had already been closed by the Worcester and Somerset Railroad constructed in 1871 and 1872 as a branch extending from "Peninsula Junction" on the ESRR to the north bank of the Pocomoke River, which might have been a first step in the realization of the link that John W. Crisfield had proposed a decade earlier between his ESRR and the newly chartered but never built Accomack and Northampton Air Line Railroad in Virginia. The general journal of the Philadelphia, Wilmington and Baltimore Railroad listed the Worcester and Somerset as a "subsidiary railroad" and reported its revenue and payments for the use of PWB rolling stock.

In November 1875, the PWB's general journal noted that the Worcester and Somerset had been leased to a man named W. Painter. On November 16, the *Philadelphia Inquirer* elaborated, "Mr. William Painter, broker, of this city, into whose hands the Worcester and Somerset Railroad, a branch from the Eastern Shore Railroad, recently passed, is working up the proposed extension of the road from its present terminus to Cherrystone, opposite Norfolk. A survey of the extension has already been made." Painter was a member of a Pennsylvania family of entrepreneurs. His brother, Uriah Hunt Painter, had won considerable acclaim as a Civil War correspondent for the *Inquirer* and was well connected in Washington, D.C. William's letters to his brother on Worcester and Somerset Railroad letterhead dating from 1876 and 1877, housed at the Historical Society of Pennsylvania, tended to dwell on continued financial difficulties in operating the W&S, so during those years, nothing more got done about extending the little branch farther south.

In 1878, William Painter's proposed extension project got a new lease on life and the new name Peninsula Railroad Company of Virginia. Both Painter brothers were elected to the original board of directors, and William Painter became the new railroad's president. Subscription books were opened on May 29, 1878, at the Accomack Courthouse in Virginia, and the project picked up some new subscribers.

Yet little more apparently happened in 1878, according to the minutes of the railroad's annual meeting held on January 20, 1879, which reported,

"The president stated that nothing of importance had been done since the last meeting, as satisfactory arrangements for completing the line when commenced were not perfected." It was another year before the minutes recorded, "The president reported that a corps of engineers would commence immediately." Whatever those engineers accomplished in 1880, the following January, a newly elected board member requested that the incoming board members "exert themselves to complete the road, getting it well underway this year." In January 1882, William Painter, still serving as president, defended the railroad's progress to date by explaining, "The corps of engineers engaged in May 1881 have been continually employed surveying and we expect the line will be permanently located at an early date. This portion of our work and everything else appertaining to this Company's interests have progressed as rapidly as was consistent." At the same meeting, the president was authorized to make contracts, to interchange business with other concerns, to obtain rights of way and to sell stocks and bonds.

In the meantime, in April 1880, the Worcester and Somerset Railroad was reorganized as the Peninsula Railroad Company of Maryland, shortly receiving authorization from the State of Maryland to extend its existing tracks across the Pocomoke River to the Maryland-Virginia state line. William Painter was elected president with his brother Uriah Hunt Painter on the board.

During the course of 1882, the two separate Peninsula Railroads became one. That February, Virginia passed legislation allowing the Peninsula Railroad Company of Virginia to receive the property and rights of the Peninsula Railroad Company of Maryland (formerly the Worcester and Somerset Railroad) and, once consolidated, to change the name of these enterprises to the New York, Philadelphia and Norfolk Railroad Company. At a special meeting of the board of directors of the Peninsula Railroad Company of Virginia, held in May 1882, the merger and consolidation of stocks, capital and properties was formally agreed to. The new railroad's headquarters would be in Drummondtown, Virginia, which was at that time the official name of the town where the Accomack County courthouse was located. The new railroad's board would have seven directors, including Uriah Hunt Painter and William Painter. Once again, William Painter was made president by the board. By September 1882, Richmond's *Daily Dispatch* reported that construction of the new railroad had actually commenced and quoted the *Eastville* (Virginia) *Herald*: "The company is in earnest about the work, and states that the prospective road from Pocomoke City to Cherrystone, Va. will make an air line from Florida to Maine."

In his letter to George Roberts on September 1881, Milton Courtright described the current state of Norfolk's economy, a subject he was quite familiar with, having been one of the builders of the Chesapeake and Albemarle Canal. "Norfolk is now the terminus of extensive lines of communication, both water and rail," he wrote. "The territory tributary to the Albemarle and Chesapeake Canal alone is equal in area to that of Massachusetts and Connecticut combined. The value of products and merchandise passing through it last year was seven to eight million dollars.... Norfolk is now I believe the third cotton port, its general commerce is large and rapidly increasing."

The Civil War had certainly disrupted the city's commerce and finances, broken up those railroads constructed during the 1850s that terminated in Norfolk and left its streets in a state of disrepair that reflected the impoverishment of its citizens. But in the ensuing decade and a half, the city largely recovered. By the 1880s, ferries and trains were once again terminating in Norfolk, and people were moving in and investing capital. The city's postwar rail connections, specifically with the Norfolk and Western and the Seaboard and Roanoke railroads, ensured that its wharves were loaded not just with local truck produce and North Carolina's lumber and tar but also coal from West Virginia and cotton from the Deep South, not to mention the newly popular foodstuff of peanuts. Norfolk even had a city railroad—a horsecar system that made it easier for folks to get around town. While it might not have actually constituted a link in a Maine to Florida rail system, the NYP&N could definitely link the urban centers of the Northeast with the producers of the South through the city of Norfolk.

The New York, Philadelphia and Norfolk Railroad is frequently described as the brainchild of William L. Scott, who is said to have begun planning such a project in the late 1870s, though his name was never associated with the Worcester and Somerset Railroad or the Peninsula Railroad of Virginia during these early years.

William L. Scott was born on July 2, 1828, in Washington, D.C., where his father was stationed as a colonel in the army. He attended Virginia schools and became a page in the U.S. House of Representatives to support himself when his parents died. Congressman Charles Reed of Erie, Pennsylvania, was sufficiently impressed to give Scott a position as a shipping clerk on the wharves he owned in that city where Scott first became interested in commerce and shipping.

By the age of twenty-three, Scott was in the shipping business for himself in Erie, and by 1871, Scott had formed the W.L. Scott Company, which

William Lawrence Scott was one of NYP&N's founders. *Erie County, Pennsylvania Historical Society.*

became one of the nation's largest coal shippers. Scott also became president of several banks and a broker on the New York Stock Exchange. Scott's political career began with his election as mayor of Erie in 1866. He was elected to the U.S. House of Representatives in 1884 and 1886, after having served as a district delegate to the Democratic National Convention and a state representative in the Democratic National Committee.

Scott's involvement with railroads began in 1853, when he married into a family with railroad interests. Scott was never directly employed by the Pennsylvania Railroad, but he advanced PRR interests on several occasions. He was a promoter and later president of the Erie and Pittsburgh Railroad and arranged for its lease to the Pennsy in 1870. In 1881, he leased Erie's piers and docks from the PRR and helped the PRR buy out the bondholders of the Columbus, Chicago & Indiana Central, giving the Pennsy control of this line.

The story goes that sometime early in 1880, Scott met with officials of the Pennsylvania Railroad Company to secure their support and backing for a north–south railroad down the Eastern Shore of the Chesapeake Bay, but no one was interested except for Alexander J. Cassatt, the brilliant engineer who could envision a bigger and better project, including car floats and tugboats big and powerful enough to make possible the world's longest ferrying operation of loaded boxcars.

Conversely, Francis Barksdale's 1901 article on Cassatt, which was probably based on an interview with him, credits Cassatt with the idea for the New York, Philadelphia and Norfolk Railroad. In this article, Cassatt approaches Scott to suggest, "Let's build a railroad from Delmar to Cape Charles, and connect with Norfolk and Portsmouth by boat." According to Barksdale, Scott was the skeptical one.

The *Centennial History of the Pennsylvania Railroad*, published in 1946 by George H. Burgess and Miles C. Kennedy, stated, "The New York, Philadelphia and Norfolk Railroad Company was promoted by Thomas A. Scott and A.J. Cassatt, at that time President and Second Vice President, respectively, of the Pennsylvania Railroad," noting that on Tom Scott's death, "Mr. Cassatt carried on alone." Historians have since attributed the mention of Tom Scott to simple confusion because he and William L. Scott shared a last name. However, the *Centennial History* was based on a comprehensive study of the origins and development of the PRR through the company's official records and those of its subsidiaries, as well as contemporary railroad and financial journals. The *Centennial History* has not been known to be fraught with errors. And Tom Scott's promotion of the failed Southern Railway Security Corporation certainly demonstrated his interest in extending the influence of the PRR in the South.

In any case, by 1880, the idea of a north–south railroad down the Eastern Shore with a ferry connection to Norfolk was hardly a new one, and plans, at least, for such an operation, namely the Painter brothers' Peninsula Railroads, were already underway.

The first actual surviving document linking the names of William L. Scott and Alexander J. Cassatt to the proposed north–south Delmarva railroad is a handwritten draft for a traffic agreement presently filed in the miscellaneous correspondence of the Philadelphia, Wilmington and Baltimore Railroad housed at the Hagley Museum and Library in Wilmington, Delaware. The document carries a handwritten note from John P. Green, an assistant to the PRR president, to William L. Scott, dated November 19, 1881. It reads, "My dear Sir, I promised Mr. Cassatt to show you this but it slipped my memory. Will you look it over and let him hear from you? Please be careful of it as I do not know that we have another copy." A document in the Uriah Hunt Painter Papers at the Chester County Historical Society, dated August 24, 1881, indicates that the same John P. Green had already shared the draft with "Mr. Painter" for his input.

If the document indeed reached Scott in November 1881, that would have been about nine months after the Pennsy rather suddenly gained control of the Philadelphia, Wilmington and Baltimore Railroad and a time when both John P. Green and Alexander J. Cassatt both became members of the PRR board. It would also have been not long after engineers began surveying a route for the Peninsula Railroad of Virginia and that railroad's board members authorized its president to make contracts to interchange business with other railroads. Scott, Cassatt and other PRR executives might well have discussed a railroad running the length of the Eastern Shore with a ferry connection to Norfolk at some earlier time, but it must have been PRR's abrupt acquisition of the PWB, which brought them the Delaware Railroad, that made taking control of the extension south an opportunity too good to miss.

The drafted traffic agreement names as participants the Pennsylvania Railroad; the Philadelphia, Wilmington and Baltimore Railroad Company; the Delaware Railroad; and the "Peninsula Railroad Company," without specifying whether it meant the Peninsula Railroad Company of Maryland or Virginia, but the terms of the agreement make it clear that the Peninsula Railroad of Virginia was the intended participant. The document acknowledges that the said Peninsula Railroad proposed to construct its tracks from "Newton Junction" to a harbor "at or near Cherrystone Inlet" in Northampton County, Virginia. The Maryland town now known as Pocomoke City had been called Newtown from 1865 until 1878, so the document was specifying territory in both Maryland and Virginia and seems to imply that the two then-separate Peninsula Railroads were already intended to become one. The harbor at or near Cherrystone Inlet implies that the "boat service for passengers and freight" to Norfolk also mentioned in the document was probably not going to be an existing ferry at a place known as Cherrystone.

The document is a traffic agreement among the several parties for freight and passenger business carried over their connecting lines between Norfolk, Virginia, and New York City. Each railroad would agree to furnish its share of cars and actively promote the service. Southbound rates for traffic originating at points north and east of Philadelphia would be fixed by PRR. Southbound rates for traffic originating in Philadelphia or points on the PWB line would be fixed by PWB. Northbound rates for traffic originating in Norfolk or points south and west, as well as traffic from any station on the Peninsula Railroad, would be fixed by the Peninsula Railroad, providing that PWB didn't end up with less revenue between Philadelphia and Baltimore than it was getting at the time.

The document's two references to the Eastern Shore Railroad Company were crossed out, probably because PWB already had plans in place to get back its control over this enterprise.

The final version of the agreement was dated May 23, 1882. In spirit, it was much the same as the 1881 draft, with a few additions and clarifications. It specifically mentioned that the Peninsula Railroad Company of Virginia and the Peninsula Railroad Company of Maryland were "to be consolidated as the New York, Philadelphia and Norfolk Railroad Company." It stated that the connection being formed would lie between "a harbor at or near Cherrystone Inlet" and Delmar, not Newton Junction, and it made it clear that the combined Peninsula Railroad Companies would be providing "a good and suitable steamboat service between the southern terminus of their line and Norfolk." All parties were exhorted to provide vehicles that could run at a reasonable speed to carry the line's anticipated "perishable property." The Pennsy and PWB agreed to construct no competing lines on the peninsula and promote no business on any competing lines that might be constructed by others, though anyone currently doing business with the Eastern Shore Railroad could continue to do so. The final agreement was signed by William Painter on behalf of the Peninsula Railroad Companies, A.J. Cassatt as the vice president of the PWB and George Roberts for the Pennsylvania Railroad Company.

There's another popular story that during the summer of 1882, Cassatt traveled south to Pocomoke City, where he proceeded on horseback to Cape Charles to personally inspect the terrain for the proposed railroad prior to making any investment or commitment. During his journey, he resisted pleas from local individuals to route the railroad through or close to their respective communities, deciding instead on tracks that would run straight down the center of the peninsula.

The Cassatt family letters housed at the Philadelphia Museum of Art hint that Cassatt was contemplating leaving the PRR in 1880, and he did request a leave of absence to visit his family in Europe that summer. In February 1882, following the PRR takeover of the PWB, and at about the same time that the two Peninsula Railroad Companies were authorized to consolidate, Cassatt's mother wrote, "In your last letter you say nothing about resigning. Have you given up the idea?" In April 1882, she wrote, "I hope you may stick to your present intentions of resigning for I am persuaded that 21 years of the kind of life you have led is quite enough for a person of a nervous temperament such as yours." On June 8, 1882, the *Philadelphia Inquirer* acknowledged rumors that Cassatt might retire, adding, "But nothing definite was positively known about the matter." Cassatt's journey south might well have been a break taken for fact finding in order to make up his mind about his future.

Cassatt probably traveled by train as far south as he could, which would have placed him in Pocomoke City and not too far from two roughly parallel roads leading south from the Maryland town of Snow Hill. Either one would have taken him to the port of Onancock, the more easterly route through Drummondtown. Proceeding farther south, he might have passed through Bell Haven and Eastville, eventually ending his trip at Cape Charles.

He might well have had to contend with local advice, but the route of the NYP&N had already been surveyed. There is no record of the surveys made for the Peninsula Railroad of Virginia in 1880 and 1881, but it's logical to think that the railroad engineers might have known about and examined a route that had been mapped in 1855 for a never-built New York and Norfolk Air Line Railway. A copy of the map resides in the collection of the Library of Virginia, which clearly shows that the plan at that time was for a north–south route that ran in a straight line south from the Virginia-Maryland border, bypassing the existing towns of Horntown and Temperanceville, and narrowly skirting Drummondtown. The proposed railroad was planned to enter Bell Haven and Hadlock en route to Eastville, where it was to split into two branches—one proceeding south to the geographical Cape Charles and the other veering west to a point identified as Steamboat Landing on a point of land between the mouths of Cherrystone Creek and King's Creek.

Regardless of whether Cassatt was traipsing down the Eastern Shore during the summer of 1882, Uriah Hunt Painter's chief engineer, E.W. Goerke, was engaged in much more than mere inspection. The letterbooks of Uriah Hunt Painter, housed at the Historical Society of Pennsylvania, contain many letters from Goerke to Painter describing his difficulty in securing rights of way and obtaining labor necessary to cut down trees and remove stumps, the initial step in grading a railroad. In the late nineteenth century, residents of underserved rural areas were often willing to simply donate the needed land, but in a letter dated June 5, 1882, Goerke wrote that some were resisting, saying that they "do not put any valuation on their land, they merely have a vague idea that 'they ought to be paid.'" On September 11, he mentioned the complicating factor that property boundaries in Eastern Shore Virginia were often a matter of "tradition and recollection" rather than records on paper. He was at that time often in the county courthouses dealing with those looking for "reassessments" on deals thought to have been made. In 1883, the NYP&N would begin paying the nominal sum of one

Uriah Hunt Painter was instrumental in the NYP&N's construction and long served on its board. *Chester County Historical Society.*

dollar to landowners for the rights of way through their properties, on the condition that the land would revert back to its original owners should the railroad ever cease its services.

The popular story continues that Cassatt made the decision to bypass Cherrystone Creek and King's Creek for a spot a mile and a half south of King's Creek, where he found a tidal creek called Mud Creek. There was no body of water named Mud Creek on the 1855 map; indeed, there was no indication of any natural feature such as a creek or an inlet where the NYP&N terminus would eventually be constructed, so the location of the NYP&N harbor might well have been an arbitrary choice of Cassatt's. The NYP&N did not run through Eastville either, so the southernmost portion of the route of the NYP&N might also have been influenced by Cassatt, maybe so that the railroad would treat the two county seats in Virginia equally by bypassing both of them.

In mid-September 1882, just as the two Peninsula Railroads were formally united and while the *Baltimore Sun* was reporting that work on the NYP&N had actually started, the Philadelphia press announced the retirement of Alexander J. Cassatt from the Pennsylvania Railroad. The Philly papers were united in their praise for this man. The *North American* called him "one of the great representative railroad men of his day.' The *Philadelphia Times* reported, "He has fairly earned the distinction of the ablest master of transportation on the continent." The *Evening Telegraph* added, "The [PRR] presidency could hardly have given him honors greater than he had already won."

The *Philadelphia Times* also noted, "He retires...without ever having entertained the thought of transferring his ripe experience to any other corporation." And throughout the rest of 1882, it probably seemed that way. Cassatt left for Europe with his family that November, leaving Scott to deal with the issue of actually funding the construction of the fledgling New York, Philadelphia and Norfolk Railroad Company.

Building a railroad is expensive. Once the surveys are done and rights of way are obtained for the land along the route, actual construction usually starts with the necessary bridges, trestles, tunnels and cuts. Then the entire route has to be graded before tracks are laid. Somewhere or other, the railroad needs engine houses and shops for the maintenance of its vehicles and offices for its administrative employees. The railroad also needs freight and passenger stations along its route, turntables at its terminals and possibly waterfront structures if the route terminates at a port. All that construction work needs to be completed by contractors who expect to be paid for their labor long before the railroad acquires any rolling stock and can start earning money by moving freight and people from place to place.

In the earliest days of railroading, once a railroad had been granted a state charter permitting it to exist, its promoters would begin to sell the concept of economic advantage through better transportation, usually through a printed prospectus or local media like newspapers. The railroad's charter might name commissioners, usually prominent citizens, who would receive subscriptions for shares of stock. Promoters might try to encourage the sale of stock subscriptions with public meetings featuring speakers and other entertainment. Even those who did not attend the meetings would read about them in the newspapers.

As railroading projects grew more ambitious and therefore more expensive, promoters might look to state and local governments for subsidies. Those governments had quickly learned that issuing subsidies to independent railroad companies was far better than trying to construct and then operate a government-run transportation system, and they could sometimes claim a share of a railroad's profits if the venture proved to be lucrative. Individuals could also subsidize railroad construction with donations of land, labor or materials, such as lumber. Many farmers contributed in this way, hoping for better access to markets for their farm produce.

By the time construction started on the NYP&N, it had become customary to capitalize railroad construction through the sale of bonds. Unlike a stockholder who owned a share of a corporation and might hope for a dividend once its operation became profitable, a bondholder was a creditor, or investor, who expected the principal he was lending to be repaid at a predetermined and competitive rate of interest. Banks sometimes became railroad bondholders, advancing capital for a railroad project after thoroughly investigating the railroad's chance of success. Banks also sometimes acted as financial agents for railroad projects by putting a railroad's stock on sale at a major financial center, such as New York City.

It was greatly to the advantage of those proposing to build a railroad to be able to get their needed capital by selling all their securities to a single buyer so that funds would be easily available when contractors needed to be paid. A bank might contract to buy an entire issue of securities at a specific date and price and then resell them as profitably as it could, absorbing the loss if they had to hold the bonds for a long time or sell them at a loss. This practice was called underwriting. Depending on a project's perceived risk, a bank might join with other banks or institutions, forming what was then known as a syndicate in order to spread out the risk. Sometimes, American railroad promoters sought capital from banks in foreign financial capitals like London or Amsterdam. In any case, by the end of the nineteenth and beginning of the twentieth centuries, capitalists and their affiliated banks generally determined which railroads got constructed.

Needless to say, the business of building railroads presented plenty of opportunities for folks who wanted to get rich quick. Some promoters financed railroad construction on bonds alone and issued all of the railroad's stock to themselves. They could declare enormous dividends on a heavily mortgaged railroad, thus bumping up the perceived value of the stock they owned, which they could then unload at a profit while they let the railroad go bankrupt. Promoters could lobby state and local governments for favorable charters, concessions of land and large cash subsidies, allocating construction work to their cronies who built as cheaply as possible. Then they could market the railroad's stocks and bonds and walk away, leaving a substandard railroad with no hope of paying the interest on its bonds or ever making enough money to issue stock dividends.

While the Pennsylvania Railroad was limited by its charter to constructing railroads in Pennsylvania, it extended its reach and built its empire by acquiring other railroads, like the PWB, but also by financially assisting in the construction of connecting lines. For example, the PRR might buy a lot of a proposed railroad's stock or endorse its bonds, as it did in the case of the Philadelphia and Erie Railroad, where it bought over three-fourths of the railroad's bond issue. In return, the PRR usually required a traffic agreement.

At a special meeting of stockholders of the New York, Philadelphia and Norfolk Railroad Company held December 11, 1882, it was resolved that the railroad needed cash and would seek to borrow the needed capital for construction. That same month, the minutes of a PRR board meeting disclosed that William L. Scott, representing the NYP&N, had already met with the PRR president, announcing that he proposed to issue $1.65 million of bonds and $1.68 million of common stock for a capitalization of $40,000 per mile of railroad. He proposed to give PRR a portion of the stocks and bonds in exchange for a traffic agreement. By September 1883, the NYP&N had an agreement with PWB and PRR in which PRR and PWB would devote 20 percent of revenue from traffic interchanged with NYP&N to payment on the interest of NYP&N's bonds. In return, NYP&N would construct a railroad to PRR standards, which would be ready for traffic no later than June 1, 1885. The agreement was signed by G.B. Roberts of the Pennsylvania Railroad Company; Frank Thomson of the Philadelphia, Wilmington and Baltimore Railroad; and Uriah Hunt Painter of the New York, Philadelphia and Norfolk Railroad Company.

So, the Pennsy did not exactly build the NYP&N, but it assisted in making cash available by guaranteeing its bonds. Other private, prominent NYP&N investors included William L. Scott, Alexander J. Cassatt, his brother J. Gardner Cassatt and Frank Thomson, who was also a PRR vice president who would become PRR president in 1897.

The letterbooks of Uriah Hunt Painter, housed at the Historical Society of Pennsylvania, contain a letter from Painter to Cassatt, dated October 7, 1884, in which Painter was complaining about who was going to be issued how many first mortgage bonds. He mentioned that back in 1881 and 1882, it had been decided that while Scott would be selling securities to complete the railroad, it also had been agreed that Painter would be issued sufficient first mortgage bonds to reimburse him for the cash he had already spent on the road during those years. There was no record of how this disagreement had been resolved, but the letter demonstrates that Painter had made an important and necessary investment early in the history of the NYP&N.

In 1880, the Eastern Shore Railroad was sold at foreclosure by its second mortgage bondholders and purchased by a syndicate of new bondholders who reorganized the business under a new Maryland charter and issued new bonds and stock. The minutes of a meeting held on June 10, 1880, by the ESRR's reorganized board, noted that books for the subscription of capital stock had been opened in Philadelphia, Wilmington, Salisbury and Princess Anne. The meeting was chaired by Samuel M. Felton, who had been president of the PWB from 1851 to 1865 and still served on its board of directors.

On July 28, the minutes of the PWB board meeting stated, "The [PWB] president reported that parties controlling the Eastern Shore Road have expressed a desire to lease that road to this Co. In view of the probability of making a lease to advantage, he advised that the question be looked into." The surviving board papers of the PWB housed at Hagley Museum and

Library contain a detailed sketch of the monthly revenue and expenses of the ESRR from January 1 to July 1, 1881.

On November 22, 1881, the *Baltimore Sun* reported that President Roberts of the Pennsy had visited Crisfield with other PRR officials to inspect the Eastern Shore Railroad with the idea of creating a continuous transportation line by adding it to the Delaware Railroad, which the PRR controlled through its recent takeover of the PWB. During the summer, a local paper, the *Salisbury Advertiser*, had reported the rumor that a number of Eastern Shore short lines were about to be "gobbled" by the Pennsy.

Early in 1882, the Pennsy denied everything. Under the headline "Flying Rumors," the *Philadelphia Inquirer* reported, "The Pennsylvania railroad officials deny that the company has any intention of leasing or purchasing the Eastern Shore railroad, of Maryland."

Nevertheless, by the end of September 1882, newspapers announced that William L. Scott made an offer on behalf of the PRR to purchase the ESRR by buying its bonds and stock at a discount. After the ESRR board declined, about a year passed until it received a telegram proposing a better offer from Alexander J. Cassatt, then residing in Europe with his family.

In the intervening time, newspapers like the *Baltimore Sun* reported that NYP&N engineers were making their own surveys for tracks to run from Delmar through Salisbury to Pocomoke City. Letters from engineer William Bauman on Peninsula Railroad stationery to Uriah Hunt Painter housed at the Historical Society of Pennsylvania confirm the rumors. In May 1882, Bauman reported that the ESRR seemed very dilapidated, and he was looking into the idea of a new line running south from Delmar and west around Salisbury to Pocomoke City. This kind of news might have made it clear to ESRR directors that a portion of their railroad could easily become redundant and greatly reduced in value and therefore might have changed some minds about selling, making them willing to accept Cassatt's offer.

In January 1884, local newspapers reported that the ESRR had finally been purchased in late December 1883 by a syndicate in which the most prominent capitalists included William L. Scott and Alexander J. Cassatt, who were also major investors in the New York, Philadelphia and Norfolk Railroad. Though this syndicate was described as independent, both the *Baltimore Sun* and the *Railroad Gazette* interpreted the event as the ESRR having been sold to the Pennsy.

While rumors of the ESRR takeover swirled during 1882 and 1883, public opinion changed. Instead of a local railroad being "gobbled" by a corporate giant, the *Crisfield Leader* reported in October 1883 that the folks of that town believed the sale "would be productive of good along the line of the road; that extensive improvements would be made, and new industries spring into existence, and that lower passenger and freight rates would be established." In December 1883, the *Baltimore Sun*'s Salisbury correspondent wrote, "Our people are delighted at the idea of having a fast train leave Salisbury every day, by which they can leave home in the morning, spend a few hours in Baltimore or Philadelphia, and reach home the same evening."

By June 1884, the Eastern Shore Railroad had officially been consolidated and merged into the New York, Philadelphia and Norfolk Railroad Company. That spring, the part of the ESRR between Delmar and Peninsula Junction had been re-laid with rails that met PRR standards, as had the old Worcester and Somerset Railroad. These would form the northernmost segment of the new NYP&N. The remainder of the old ESRR would become NYP&N's Crisfield Branch.

Concurrent with construction work that began in 1884, the NYP&N had a lot of behind-the-scenes administrative and organizational work to do. At the very beginning of the year, it was apparent that it would need additional time for completing the line, since it had already missed its contracted completion date, which had been the end of 1883. In January, Virginia's senate extended the completion time by two years for construction of a rail line extending from the Maryland state line to some unspecified place near Cherrystone Inlet, providing half the construction work was finished in half that time.

A proper management team had to be put in place for the railroad's construction phase. The composition of the NYP&N board during its earliest years indicates the Pennsy was keeping a close eye on its investment. In January 1884, the NYP&N directors included William L. Scott, William Painter, Uriah Hunt Painter, J. Gardner Cassatt and R.H. Townsend. Townsend was Scott's son-in-law and the business partner of J. Gardner Cassatt in a financial firm established in 1882 called Cassatt, Townsend & Co., in which William L. Scott acted as a "special partner." In May 1884, when William Painter died, he was replaced by Clement A. Griscom, today known primarily as a shipping magnate, who had been elected to the Pennsy's board of directors that year. Also joining the NYP&N board that May was William A. Patton, a PRR executive and general assistant to the PRR president, who had long worked with Alexander J. Cassatt. That same month, the *Railroad Gazette* described the NYP&N as "being controlled by parties largely interested in the PRR." Indeed, the early NYP&N board meetings were often held in Philadelphia. Alexander J. Cassatt was not yet an official member of the management team but would join the board the following year.

In January 1884, NYP&N president Uriah Hunt Painter contracted for the actual construction of the railroad with John Keller, a professional and veteran railroad builder from Pennsylvania. Later that month, after William L. Scott had been appointed president, members of the NYP&N board resolved that the Union Trust Company, holder of the railroad's first mortgage bonds, deliver $148,500 to Scott to cover the initial building expenses. By early February, the *Baltimore Sun* reported, "Sixteen car-loads of steel rails for the NYP&NRR have arrived at Delmar and are being distributed along the line."

Early in 1884, the NYP&N management team was also making plans to accommodate its prospective cargo when it reached the Western Shore at Norfolk. In March 1884, the *Baltimore Sun* reported, "The use of the extensive terminal facilities of the Norfolk and Western Railroad Company at Norfolk has been offered to the New York, Philadelphia and Norfolk Railroad Company." In September, the *Sun* continued, "The [NYP&N] railroad company, it is stated, have leased the wharf and warehouse property at Norfolk known as Smith's on Town Point."

Pretty much all railroad historians agree that Alexander J. Cassatt was in charge of the construction of the NYP&N. Yet while the Cassatt family did return from Europe by Christmas of 1883, early in 1884, the family set off to tour the American West by train and then returned to Europe in the fall. But there is evidence that Cassatt was staying informed at a distance. The letterbooks of Uriah Hunt Painter, housed at the Historical Society of Pennsylvania, contain more than one letter from E.W. Goerke to Painter, informing him that he had also submitted progress reports to a "Mr. Cassatt." On May 15, 1884, Goerke wrote Painter that since his last report, Mr. Cassatt had requested a change, thus the line's "location slightly deviates" from the initial plan. Two weeks before that, in a letter dated April 29, 1884, Goerke told Painter that "Mr. Scott" had also requested a change.

A letter housed at the Philadelphia Museum of Art, written by J. Gardner Cassatt, the railroad's official treasurer and member of its executive and financial committee, to his brother Alexander informed Alexander J. Cassatt about various checks he had written and signed for construction work. In November 1884, Alexander J. Cassatt's name appears for the first time in the NYP&N official board minutes, which list him as an "agent" receiving capital stock for funds due John Keller for construction work.

By early spring in 1884, Eastern Shore residents could see for themselves that the railroad was making progress in construction work at a relatively rapid pace. A Salisbury newspaper noted that John Keller was sending down carloads of Italian immigrant laborers who would be housed in shanties while they worked. By the end of May 1884, the NYP&N had completed the construction of its first major engineering feature: a bridge across the Pocomoke River. The *Baltimore Sun* reported on May 27, "A train for the first time passed over it Saturday.…The crossing of the bridge by the train was celebrated by the blowing of all the whistles of the mills and factories, and by firing a cannon salute. The banks of the river were crowded with people, including many ladies."

By early June, the route had been graded from Pocomoke City to a point near the Accomack County courthouse in Virginia. The *Baltimore Sun* reported that the railroad's laborers were expected to lay a half to a mile of track daily with the grading crew keeping ahead of the track laying crew to prevent delays. By early August, a passenger train carrying Keller and a number of other NYP&N senior employees traveled from Pocomoke City to where the railroad skirted Drummondtown, and within another month, NYP&N rails extended to Pungoteague, a point seven miles south of the railroad's new Accomack Station.

Back in 1883, the NYP&N board authorized its president (then Uriah Hunt Painter) to contract for a telegraph line to be constructed parallel to its intended railroad. During the Civil War, the Eastern Shore of Virginia had briefly enjoyed telegraph service thanks to a military telegraph line extending from Princess Anne to Cherrystone. However, this line had been used mainly for government communication and had been strung from slender pine saplings that rotted from disease after the war. In September 1884, the *Baltimore Sun* announced, "The telegraph line on the New York, Philadelphia and Norfolk Railroad has been completed as far as Accomac [*sic*] Station,

This 1890 photo shows the tracks of the NYP&N, which ran for miles in a straight line down the center of Virginia's eastern shore. *Cape Charles Historical Society, Photograph Collection.*

about 30 miles below Pocomoke City, and the people of the Eastern Shore of Virginia are now enabled for the first time since the country was founded to communicate with the outer world by electricity."

Despite delays caused by rails and ties occasionally not reaching the construction site when needed and laborers walking off the job when tracks needed to be laid in swampy areas, on October 25, E.W. Goerke, the railroad's construction engineer, telegraphed Uriah Hunt Painter that construction work had reached the railroad's intended terminus, at that time a field within sight of the Chesapeake Bay. On November 17, 1884, the NYP&N officially opened for cargo and passengers. Announcements about this "New Line to Norfolk" appeared in Philadelphia and Trenton newspapers. Even the prestigious *New York Times* predicted, "The new road will make contributory to New York a large and wealthy section of country which has hitherto given its patronage to other sections. Garden truck and fish and oysters will form a considerable portion of the freight."

In December, the *Philadelphia Inquirer* interviewed NYP&N vice president William A. Patton, who stated that the railroad's executives hoped the line would become a critical link between the nation's North and South. Patton said, "Much of the Southern trade belongs to Philadelphia and we will do all we can to get it back....Naturally that trade should seek the shortest line of communication, and since the railroad has been built that line has been

One of the earliest images of a NYP&N locomotive, captured in 1884. *Cape Charles Historical Society, Photograph Collection.*

provided….A man can go from Philadelphia to Norfolk about as quick as he can go from Philadelphia to Altoona."

A few days before the official opening of the NYP&N, a gentleman from Middletown, Delaware, organized a southbound rail excursion consisting of about one hundred farmers and real estate brokers occupying two passenger cars. The party included some of Delaware's most influential citizens, and their mission was to scout out land on the eastern shore of Virginia with value that was certain to rise thanks to newly available rail service. The speculators' train stopped in Pocomoke City, where the local hotel was incapable of accommodating so large a crowd, but according to the *Baltimore Sun*, "The hospitable citizens of that place came forward and offered to take the balance." The following day, a special engine was attached to their cars, and their train stopped at the NYP&N's new stations, including those named Metompkin "in the heart of the sweet potato region"; Accomack, which had been constructed between the existing towns of Onancock and Drummondtown; Pungoteague; Bell Haven; and Eastville, where the new depot was still under construction about a quarter mile away from the town of the same name, which was the seat of Northampton County. When the train arrived at the railroad's terminus, the passengers disembarked to observe heavy machinery dredging a harbor and wharves still under construction. Since there was yet no steamboat service across the bay, the party spent two hours looking around and then boarded the train and returned north to spend the night in Salisbury.

A few days following the railroad's official opening, the land speculators' excursion was followed by another special train, this one carrying "a large party of officials connected with the Pennsylvania Railroad Company," according to the *Philadelphia Inquirer*, whose purpose was to inspect the line. This time, there was a steamboat waiting to take the group across the bay. They stayed overnight and banqueted at the Hygeia Hotel at Old Point Comfort and then left for Newport News, where they boarded a Chesapeake and Ohio train for Richmond. The party included George Roberts, president of the Pennsy; a number of PRR vice presidents and executives; and William L. Scott and William A. Patton, president and vice president of the NYP&N. The *Philadelphia Inquirer* named Alexander J. Cassatt as a member of the party but identified him only as a PRR director.

The vessel that took the railroad brass across the Chesapeake was called the *Jane Moseley*, and it had been making the trip to Old Point Comfort and Norfolk since the NYP&N's opening day on November 17, 1884. It was a wooden side-wheeler passenger ferry that could also handle freight but not

One of the earliest images of the station at Cape Charles City, Virginia, showing signs of continuing construction work. *Cape Charles Historical Society, Photograph Collection.*

exactly the vessel that the managers of the NYP&N had envisioned. William A. Patton had chartered it for a period of four to six months so that some sort of ferry service could be provided on opening day. Unfortunately, on December 22, the *Jane Moseley* ran aground while pulling out of the new NYP&N Eastern Shore harbor and struck an old submerged anchor, which cut a hole in its bow. The *Richmond Dispatch* reported, "She was towed into the dock by a tug and sunk. No serious damage was done, and the vessel will be raised at once." However, early in 1885, the NYP&N replaced the *Jane Moseley* with a new chartered steamer called the *Eastern Shore*, which had previously been making runs between Baltimore and Crisfield.

Meanwhile, a Wilmington firm called Harlan & Hollingsworth was building several custom vessels for the railroad. One was a powerful tugboat and the other was a large side-wheeled steamer designed to carry passengers and mail. This ship, called the *Cape Charles*, arrived on March 27, 1885. It was equipped with electric lights and capable of traveling at eighteen to twenty miles per hour. Its main deck was fitted out with two sets of railroad tracks designed to hold Pullman passenger cars, mail cars and luggage cars. The NYP&N was cooperating with other railroads to let passengers book space on a sleeping car that would leave New York City, pass through Philadelphia, cross the Chesapeake and then continue to the popular winter resort of Jacksonville, Florida. This direct through service did not prove to be as popular as expected and was discontinued in 1887. After that, passengers heading for Florida had to vacate their Pullman cars and walk onto the *Cape Charles*, but once aboard, they could enjoy the ship's elegant dining hall, social hall, well-equipped bathrooms and promenade deck.

In March 1886, Harlan & Hollingsworth supplied the NYP&N with another smaller side-wheeled steamer called the *Old Point Comfort*, this one built without the railroad tracks. On November 1, this steamer was plying a new route between the NYP&N harbor and Richmond. Those arriving at the NYP&N harbor on the morning train could be in Richmond by 6:00 p.m. The *Old Point Comfort* left Richmond the following morning and connected with NYP&N's night train, arriving in Philadelphia or New York the morning after that. The new route was popular with both passengers and freight customers, but the service came to an abrupt end when the Interstate Commerce Act was passed in 1887. New government regulation of railroad rates rendered the NYP&N's steamer-rail route unable to compete with all-water routes between the same ports, so the NYP&N ended the service in April 1887.

While the NYP&N passengers were left to transfer themselves between train and steamboat, the railroad still planned to leave the freight they were transporting in its railroad cars and ship it across the Chesapeake on car floats, also called transfer boats. The Francis Barksdale article published in 1901 made this seem like it had been solely Cassatt's idea, quoting him as having suggested to Scott: "We will build powerful and fast transfer tugs that will transport loaded trains across the bay." The concept was not really new, but car floats had previously been used primarily for short hauls within harbors and not across thirty-six miles of open water in all sorts of weather. In May 1884, the *Railroad Gazette* reported that the NYP&N had contracted for two large transfer boats. According to the board meeting minutes of both the Pennsy and the NYP&N, the Pennsylvania Railroad actually paid to have the car floats constructed and then leased them to the NYP&N. In March 1885, the vessel mundanely named *Car Float No. 1* arrived at the NYP&N Eastern Shore harbor together with a new tug called the *Norfolk*. *Car Float No. 1* was a wooden barge 224 feet long fitted with railroad tracks. On March 12, twelve freight cars were rolled on board, and the tug hauled the barge on its maiden voyage to Norfolk. The

One of the earliest images of a car float being loaded, circa 1890. *Cape Charles Historical Society, Photograph Collection.*

Richmond Dispatch reported, "She made the run, a distance of thirty-six miles, in four hours."

Watching, no doubt proudly, was the new president of the NYP&N, Alexander J. Cassatt, who had been elected by the railroad's board in February 1885. While Cassatt's elevation to this position might have been long planned by board members at both the Pennsy and the NYP&N, it does not appear to have been publicly anticipated or rumored. Various notices had appeared in *Railroad Gazette* since 1883, hinting that Cassatt would assume leadership of some other railroad, like the Denver and Rio Grande Company.

Scott had resigned his position as NYP&N president because he had been elected to the U.S. House of Representatives, but he remained on the railroad's board and continued to promote it. In a lengthy interview printed in the *Peninsula Enterprise* in April 1885, Scott said, "I am going down to Cape Charles tonight, the future city of the Peninsula…with the intention of making that the greatest oystering, fruit, and farm truck shipping point in the United States.…Then this line of railroad [intends] to put the products of the Virginia planter into Fulton Market [in New York City] just as cheap, if not cheaper, and just as quick as the Long Island trucker can make his haul."

Little over a month after *Car Float No. 1* made its maiden voyage, the local press was commenting on the railroad's success. On April 22, 1885, the *Richmond Dispatch* reported, "The new railroad down the Eastern Shore is rapidly increasing its freight and passenger traffic. More than fifteen hundred passengers went over the line during four days of last week, and the shipments of freight over the road have increased beyond the most sanguine expectations of the projectors of the enterprise." In May, the *Peninsula Enterprise* reported that the NYP&N had ordered two hundred extra freight cars and two additional transfer boats. In December, the *Richmond Dispatch* added, "On and after the 20th instant the mails will be carried over this new route, thus enabling our people to get the Richmond papers in the afternoon of the day on which they are printed."

Neither the reporters nor the land speculators who had ridden the NYP&N to its southern terminus around its opening day spent very much time in the place, because at that time, there was not too much to see. Technically, the NYP&N's terminus had been named Cape Charles City to distinguish it from the geographical Cape Charles eleven miles to the south, but at the end of 1884 and the beginning of 1885, it remained, as Scott had termed

Bushels of potatoes awaiting shipment at Cape Charles City, Virginia, 1890. *Cape Charles Historical Society, Photograph Collection.*

it, a "future city," still mainly farmland and woodland plagued with a lot of swampy patches.

At that time, much of the land belonged to William L. Scott, whose interest in real estate development matched his interest in politics and railroading. In May 1883, Scott had purchased over 2,100 acres of land from Sally and Ella Tazewell for $55,000. The purchase consisted of three separate tracts known as the Old Plantation, the New Quarter and King's Creek Plantation.

Before the month of May was over, the NYP&N's civil engineer, William Bauman, showed up to survey and topographically map the place, indicating the locations of its cleared land, wooded land, creeks, lakes and ponds. His letters to Uriah Hunt Painter from June through September 1883 reflect the difficulty of this task, particularly around King's Creek, which was crooked and densely wooded. In a letter dated May 31, 1883, Bauman mentioned the necessity of making it seem that the Tazewell purchase had nothing to do with the railroad: "Mr. Scott being the buyer and sole owner of the estate," but by July, the local tenants had figured out what was going on and were inquiring whether they would be permitted to stay on another year to farm the land they leased. By September 1883, Bauman's maps indicated the tentative future site of railroad tracks through the Tazewell purchase, and Scott soon sold forty acres of waterfront for the NYP&N's harbor and rail yard.

North of the NYP&N property, Scott had William Bauman survey and map the future Cape Charles City. About 136 acres of land would be divided into building lots, each measuring 40 by 140 feet laid out along seven east–west avenues named after Virginia politicians and six north–south streets named mainly for locally grown fruits (though there was also a Pine Street). The town's grid plan enclosed a central park. Its main business street, Mason Street, divided the town's residential section from the railroad's property so that its hotels and businesses could overlook the impressive rail yard and harbor. Scott sold Bauman two prime building lots for one dollar each.

Needless to say, the first structures to rise in Cape Charles City were built to house and feed railroad employees. The NYP&N constructed bunkhouses, and as early as the summer of 1884, Cape Charles City had its first tavern. Other taverns, hotels and boardinghouses followed with general stores, dance halls and a billiard parlor. Law enforcement became a key priority for the town's early municipal government, especially on Saturday nights when the local watermen mixed it up with the railroad workers after the various establishments closed.

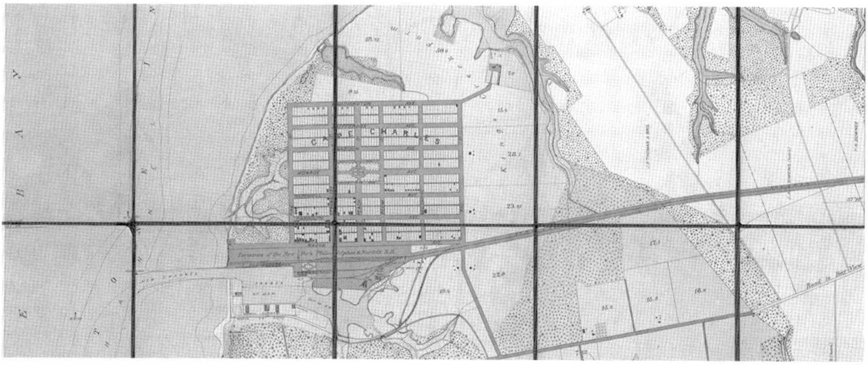

This 1887 map of William L. Scott's estate illustrates the early layout of Cape Charles City. *Eastern Shore Public Library*.

In January 1885, the *Richmond Dispatch* reported that in the town, "a large number of new houses will be completed in the early spring and many others are under contract." Many of them were built in the popular Queen Anne and Shingle styles. By the time Cape Charles City was officially incorporated in 1886, it was a fairly sophisticated place for the eastern shore of Virginia, boasting paved streets, electricity and a sewage system. Because the people who lived and worked there were a religiously diverse group, it soon had churches of many denominations, including Roman Catholic, Methodist, Episcopal, African Methodist Episcopal and Baptist.

The railroad had commenced dredging its harbor in 1883 on the site of what had been called Mud Creek, sometimes also identified as a pond, which could overflow with heavy rain or drain practically dry at very low tide. In November 1884, the *Baltimore Sun* reported, "Two immense dredges are dredging the harbor, which will be 2,500 feet long. The mud is taken in large scows and towed out into shoal water in the bay and dumped. Two tugboats are employed to do this towing….The wharves are also in course of construction." By the time the *Jane Moseley* made its maiden voyage, the railroad had a narrow channel connecting the harbor and the waters of the bay. In January 1885, the *Richmond Dispatch* reported, "The work of dredging the artificial harbor of thirty acres is going on bravely."

The same newspaper article noted, "The New York, Philadelphia and Norfolk Railroad Company are building round-houses for engines and cars at Cape Charles City. Fine depot buildings are also in process of construction." A freight shed went up between the harbor where steamboats would dock and rail platforms where passenger trains would arrive and depart. A passenger station with a ticket office and waiting room was later constructed east of the freight shed. The facilities were designed so that passengers arriving at Cape Charles City could easily move from their rail cars to waiting steamboats. Eventually, the NYP&N property at Cape Charles City had everything a rail yard needed, including water tanks and repair shops. William L. Scott's private rail siding was just south of the harbor.

Also located south of the harbor was an estate that became known as Hollywood Place or Hollywood Farm. It consisted of 1,500 acres of the Tazewell purchase that William L. Scott kept for himself, and it included the old Tazewell mansion, which he enlarged and renovated. Scott's official family residence continued to be his home in Erie, and when Congress was in session, he occupied a D.C. apartment, so it's unclear how much time he spent on his Virginia farm. However, Scott did use the place to entertain important guests like President Grover Cleveland. By the late 1880s, the *New York Times* reported that about one hundred workers were employed on the estate under the direction of Scott's on-site managers and agents. The headline of a *New York Times* article printed on August 18, 1890, called Hollywood Place "a Valuable Truck Farm," its success having been assured by its proximity to rail transportation.

Scott moved his prize racehorses from his stud farm in Erie south to Hollywood Farm, where he built a racetrack that became a central feature of the county agricultural fair, which Scott established in 1888 on grounds also located on the estate. On October 20, 1889, the *New York Times* commented, "One can sit in the grand stand and look at the horse race and a boat race at the same time, and see in the distance the big steamers going up and down the bay."

Scott didn't have much time to enjoy his Virginia plantation; he died on September 19, 1891, at the early age of sixty-three. Scott was staying in Newport, Rhode Island, at the time, recovering from some stomach disorders. Over the course of his final weekend, he suffered three heart attacks, the last one fatal. Scott was buried on September 24 in Erie, where flags flew at half-mast for this town's favorite son. Grover Cleveland attended the funeral, as did the governor of Pennsylvania. Pennsylvania Railroad president George B. Roberts was one of Scott's pallbearers. Scott was buried in a granite and marble mausoleum fifty feet high and shaped like a Greek cross. Various newspapers reported the edifice had cost Scott $50,000 and estimated his net worth as $10 to $20 million, a sum to which his Eastern Shore venture had no doubt significantly contributed.

5

The Pennsy Officially Adopts the NYP&N

The early success of the NYP&N made competition virtually inevitable. As early as February 1885, the *Richmond Dispatch* reported that a "prospecting party of engineers" had been spotted at Cape Charles City, taking soundings in the bay. The *Dispatch* noted, "Rumors have been afloat that another railroad would be built down the peninsula to serve as a feeder to the Baltimore and Ohio system, and thus divert to Baltimore the trade of this prosperous section, which since the completion of the New York, Philadelphia, and Norfolk railroad, has been drifting to the cities for which the railroad is named."

However, when the route for a competing railroad finally emerged a little over a year later, the proposed line was not planned to run parallel to the NYP&N but instead to traverse the lower eastern shore of Maryland, more or less diagonally. The Baltimore and Eastern Shore Railroad Company (B&ES) was chartered on April 1, 1886, and according to an opinion piece in the *Baltimore Sun* on the day in July when its route was announced, the new railroad was "designed to bring Baltimore into closer relations with the Eastern Shore counties." The *Sun* commented, "Philadelphia has already taken time by the forelock by reaching down into the peninsula in every direction, while Baltimore, as the Eastern Shore has grown and prospered, has been compelled to see her trade with that section drift to a large extent into other channels." The Baltimore and Eastern Shore Railroad would run west from the emerging seaside resort of Ocean City, Maryland, cross the NYP&N tracks at Salisbury and continue northwest to Claiborne on the

Chesapeake Bay. From there, ferries would conduct freight and passengers to a landing near Annapolis and then via short lines to Baltimore.

In mid-April 1886, in a news article in which the *Sun* announced the election of B&ES officers, while the railroad's route was still in the planning stages, the newspaper hinted at popular support for the project, at least in one of the Maryland counties it would traverse: "So far as Wicomico county is concerned, there will be no trouble about the right of way, the farmers being willing to give that through their land free of cost." But to reach Ocean City, the new railroad would have to take control of an existing short line called the Wicomico and Pocomoke Railroad.

The Wicomico and Pocomoke Railroad had been named for the two Eastern Shore rivers it connected. It was chartered in 1848, and its charter had been revived in 1854 following a period when nothing had been accomplished. Construction did not begin until 1867, and by 1868, the little railroad linked the towns of Salisbury and Berlin. It was extended toward Ocean City in stages, and by 1876, it reached the fledgling resort over a trestle bridge. The access it provided quickly encouraged the development of Ocean City. By that time, the Eastern Shore Railroad had connected Crisfield and Delmar via Salisbury, so it could be argued that these two railroads combined already formed a trans-peninsula line with a junction at Salisbury.

By May 1890, there was a sufficient amount of trackage on the ground for B&ES directors to host a tour of inspection for a party of Baltimore businessmen, bankers and capitalists. The group left Baltimore's Camden Station at 9:00 a.m. for Bay Ridge, where they boarded a steamer headed for Claiborne in Talbot County. When they arrived, they found Claiborne's railroad pier still under construction, so the party was transferred to shore in rowboats. General J.B. Seth, a Maryland lawyer and politician who was also president of the B&ES, met them with a locomotive and passenger car for their ride to Easton, where a new hotel was under construction, and the Choptank River, where the railroad crossed the water on a trestle bridge. They made a stop in Preston and continued to a point near Hurlock, where they watched contractors operate a track-laying machine. On the return trip, the inspecting party left the train at St. Michaels, where the group reboarded the steamer that had brought them across the bay.

Considering the speed with which the NYP&N had been constructed, it might seem curious that a railroad chartered in 1886 remained so unfinished four years later, but the B&ES had its share of financing issues, and for a time in 1887, the project had been considered dead. The railroad promoters had expected the city of Baltimore to endorse the railroad's bonds, but the city's recent investment experience in railroad stocks and bonds had made any further ventures unlikely at that time. By August 1888, things were looking up, and the *Sun* reported that the railroad's promoters "have wisely abandoned the effort to obtain the endorsement by the city of Baltimore in its municipal capacity of bonds of the company, and are relying instead upon individual subscriptions by our businessmen for the amount still needed," which amounted to $125,000.

Contractors started work during the summer of 1889, though the railroad was still short $75,000, which its promoters were hoping would be forthcoming in the form of subsidies from the Eastern Shore counties of Talbot, Caroline, Dorchester and Wicomico. In May 1890, the *Sun* revealed that two syndicates had underwritten the B&ES: one from Maryland and the other from New England. Later that year, the *Sun* added that the B&O was assisting by lending cars to support the railroad's expected traffic.

The B&ES was considered completed on September 15, 1890, but it was not until November 12 that the *Sun* announced, "With a new schedule next Monday will begin the active business of hauling freight on regular time." The B&ES had several chartered steamers, as well as its *William Claiborne*, which was 280 feet long and had passenger accommodations, plus two tracked sections that could carry four freight cars each. By that time, the railroad also had an Eastern Shore landing place. The 1,000-foot pier at Claiborne had been completed and a little village was growing around the new port, already boasting two oyster packinghouses and two stores. About a quarter mile away, the railroad had constructed its Eastern Shore engine houses, water tank and turntable.

There were big plans for the railroad's eastern terminus on the Atlantic Ocean. The Sinnepuxent Beach Company had purchased oceanfront and bayfront land from an estate and was marking off streets and erecting a boardwalk intended to spur the construction of fine hotels. By the summer of 1891, the B&ES was experimenting with a fast train that could cover the eighty-eight miles between Claiborne and Ocean City in two hours.

Though the railroad was welcomed by the farmers of the Eastern Shore's lower Maryland counties, who otherwise would have continued hauling their produce to Salisbury or Delmar, the B&ES had financial problems from the start. The railroad had borrowed considerable money for construction, and it failed to pay interest on its bonds, placing its operation in receivership from 1891. Problems like a failed peach crop in 1892 and a flood at Ocean City at the height of the 1893 summer season kept revenues down.

In 1894, rumors surfaced that the B&O Railroad and the Central Railroad of New Jersey would supply the funds to get the B&ES out of receivership, but by July 1894, the railroad's mortgage holders filed for foreclosure. On July 23, the *Sun* reported, "No bid for the road less than $400,000 will be accepted, and the purchaser must pay $100,000 cash." Who had that kind of money? On July 31, the *Philadelphia Inquirer* stated, "The city of Baltimore has become alarmed by certain signs that the Pennsylvania Railroad Company proposes to buy up the Baltimore and Eastern Shore railroad franchises."

The PRR did not make the purchase per se. The assets of the B&ES were sold at public auction on August 29, 1894, at the courthouse in Salisbury to a corporation called by its organizers the Baltimore, Chesapeake & Atlantic Railway Company (BC&A). However, its chief backers were PRR allies. A well-known Bostonian financier named John E. Searles became its first president.

In the annual report for 1895, which is contained in the board minutes of the BC&A, the corporation reported that its assets included eight locomotives, one parlor car, four excursion cars, sixteen passenger cars, forty-eight boxcars and twenty-nine gondolas. The corporation also operated eight steamer lines, among three steamboat companies serving one hundred wharves and landings on the Chesapeake and its tributary rivers. However, for the next five years, BC&A annual reports stated that the earnings of the corporation failed to meet expectations. Reasons cited included general economic depression at this time, poor crop yields and the need for repairs at its depots and on its bridges. Even as part of the extended PRR family, the BC&A never really functioned as a second main line on the Eastern Shore or enjoyed the commercial success of the NYP&N. Most folks experienced it mainly as a way to get to the Atlantic seashore.

Not long before the B&ES was sold in 1894, the *Sun* reported plans for a second trans-peninsula railroad to be constructed roughly parallel to the B&ES but slightly farther north. There had been proposals for such a railroad four years earlier, and it seemed that people were finally willing to subscribe some cash. The Queen Anne Railroad (QARR) was chartered in Maryland in 1894 and in Delaware in 1895. Heading up this enterprise was a Baltimore financier named William H. Bosley. The *Sun* editorialized on December 12, 1894, "Baltimore interests are much involved in the project, for now New York and Philadelphia get the great bulk of our produce, whereas with quick transportation, our metropolis would receive the larger share."

The Queen Anne Railroad (also sometimes known as the Queen Anne's Railroad) was constructed in stages, and once again, compared with the construction of the NYP&N, the work proceeded at an extremely slow pace. On August 12, 1896, the *Sun* reported that its tracks to Denton would be completed in "only a few weeks," though the town was already enjoying one of the benefits of rail transportation: "There has been a noticeable demand for building lots and houses." On April 3, 1897, the *Sun* announced, "There will be two trains daily each way between Queenstown and Greenwood, Del., the present eastern terminus of the line." On May 17, 1897, the *Philadelphia Inquirer* reported that construction of the railroad had overcome a major obstacle: "The trouble between the Delaware Railroad Company and the Queen Anne Railroad Company over the crossing of the tracks of the former road by the latter, at Greenwood, has been settled, and the new road will now be pushed forward to completion as rapidly as possible." The railroad was finally completed to Lewes, Delaware, in March 1898. The railroad later acquired trackage rights into Delaware's seaside resort of Rehoboth.

Starting in 1897, the Queen Anne Railroad tried to establish rail-steamer service to the older and more popular Jersey resort of Cape May. Within a few more years, it had this route up and running, but it never met with full approval or support from the Pennsy, whose management preferred that folks get to Cape May over the rails they controlled through New Jersey. In 1901, the railroad constructed a six-mile branch to Centreville, and the following year, it moved its western terminus from Queenstown to Love Point on Kent Island, which had a better harbor and shortened the ferry ride to Baltimore. However, this trans-Delmarva railroad also failed to live up to expectations. The Queen Anne became a less popular route across the peninsula to a less popular Atlantic shore resort.

While Baltimore business interests tried to compete with the NYP&N, the railroad's management under the leadership of Alexander J. Cassatt focused on improvements designed to make it a more formidable foe. Before the decade of the 1880s ended, it had become clear that the most crucial of such improvements would be made across the bay around Norfolk.

The original NYP&N Norfolk terminal was located at the western end of Norfolk's Main Street. By early 1887, the railroad's board meeting minutes show that its managers were negotiating for new wharf property. They soon constructed a new terminal at the foot of Brooke Avenue that was shared with the C&O Railroad. NYP&N vice president William A. Patton was quoted in the board minutes of January 1888, declaring the railroad's Norfolk terminal facilities were then "second to none," but they soon proved to be inadequate for the steady growth of Norfolk. In a first-person travel

The early success of the NYP&N sparked construction of two trans-Delmarva railroads. *Queen Anne's Railroad Society.*

account published in the *Times* on October 11, 1887, the unnamed author opined that Norfolk had finally "awakened" following the Civil War, thanks to "northern energy and capital." Rail connections to the west and south enhanced its trade, while the NYP&N, its chief connection to the north, facilitated its main export of oysters and produce.

By the mid-1890s, eight railroads terminated in Norfolk, each with its own water terminal. NYP&N tugs and car floats had to call at each one of them to transfer freight cars, while also negotiating heavy harbor traffic created by passenger ferries, as well as steamships bound for other northern and southern ports. On November 1, 1895, *Railroad Gazette* published an article titled "Car Ferries," mentioning that the previous year, NYP&N barges had moved 36,772 boxcars, counting freight moving in both directions.

The NYP&N board meeting minutes indicate that Cassatt et al had been considering a Norfolk "beltline" as early as 1887. This would be a short line railroad circling Norfolk and connecting a NYP&N Norfolk terminal with the city's other major carriers. It would essentially replace tugboats herding car floats around the harbor with locomotives interchanging freight cars on dry land. It was not until January 1896 that Cassatt got the NYP&N's Virginia charter amended to allow for construction of a beltline. By July of that year, the *Norfolk Virginian* announced that the NYP&N had purchased thirty-five acres of land on the Portsmouth side of the Elizabeth River.

An article printed in the *Portsmouth News* on February 9, 1897, hinted at the possible reason for the delay. The article was titled "Will Change Things," and it stated, "Years ago Portsmouth businessmen rushed to the Legislature to oppose the chartering of a belt line, fearful that it meant the diversion of railroad business passing through this city to Norfolk. Now all this is changed and the people of Portsmouth with the vast and extending system of the Seaboard, the Atlantic Coast Line through the Norfolk and Carolina, and the extensive Southern railway system, which include the three greatest railway systems in the South, within her doors, feels safe in welcoming the building of this belt line."

In November 1896, the *Norfolk Virginian* published a brief article titled "Capitalists in Norfolk," stating that Alexander J. Cassatt, William A. Patton and Clement A. Griscom of the NYP&N had arrived in town to meet with a Mr. Watson Dickerman of the Norfolk & Southern Railroad. The reason for the meeting was not explained, but it was probably a planning session for the proposed beltline.

Cassatt had originally planned for the NYP&N to construct and operate the proposed beltline, but after considering the beltline's estimated cost and the current finances of his own railroad, Cassatt decided that a better approach would be an independent beltline jointly owned by the NYP&N and the seven other railroads it would connect with. Cassatt met with the presidents of the Norfolk & Western Railroad, the Chesapeake & Ohio Railroad, the Southern Railway Company, the Atlantic & Danville Railroad, the Atlantic Coast Line, the Norfolk & Southern Railroad and the Seaboard Air Line Railroad. After resolving a few issues, he got them all to sign a formal agreement in July 1897. Each railroad subscribed to an equal share of the beltline's capital, and each named its own director to the beltline's board.

The new company's directors met in New York at the end of September 1897 and authorized construction to begin on the new Norfolk and Portsmouth Belt Line Railroad. On September 26, 1898, the first beltline train ran, and the area in Virginia known as Hampton Roads entered a new era of tremendously improved efficient and flexible railroad operation.

The same day, NYP&N opened its new Port Norfolk terminal and yard at the northern terminus of the beltline, where it had been purchasing property piecemeal for some time. By November 1898, the NYP&N transferred all its local freight business to Port Norfolk.

While the board meeting minutes of the NYP&N recorded profits in the railroad's net earnings from 1887, the decade of the 1890s was not a particularly good one for the American railroad industry. So many rail lines had been constructed that railroads had to compete for freight traffic, which kept their revenues down. Large shippers demanded special rates by threatening to ship their freight via a competing railroad. Railroads sometimes responded by forming pools to make and enforce rates in designated areas, but these associations were declared illegal by the Sherman Antitrust Act of 1890.

The Pennsy's annual report for 1897 printed in *Railroad Gazette* on March 4, 1898, acknowledged that following a poor year for the railroad's business in 1896, business had improved during the first half of 1897, but expenses had also risen, eating up PRR's gross revenue and causing "retrenchments" to be "pushed farther than before." The railroad experienced additional turbulence when its youthful president, Frank Thomson, died in 1899 after serving only two years in office.

While net earnings grew at the NYP&N, Cassatt had long ago foreseen that his new venture would need a special long-term relationship with the Pennsy. Back in 1888, on December 7, he had written to PRR president George Roberts, "It is probable that net revenues will not for some time to come, be sufficient to pay the interest on the 1st. Mortgage Bonds." Cassatt requested that the PRR and the PWB help the NYP&N by setting aside for five years from 1890 10 percent of the gross receipts from traffic between Delmar and New York from all business interchanged with the NYP&N to create a fund to purchase coupons from bondholders who might want to sell them. In return, the NYP&N would apply all net revenue after expenses to pay for the overdue coupons held and the interest thereon. The NYP&N would issue no stock dividends until all such coupons were paid. Cassatt's letter, currently housed in the PWB board files at Hagley Museum and Library, ended with the paragraph, "If the above request be granted we would further ask your companies to agree, however, not to cause legal proceedings, looking to the foreclosure and sale of the corporate property and franchises of the N.Y.P.&N. R.R. Co., to be instituted upon said coupons for a period of fifteen years from the date of the contract of September 26th, 1883 unless such proceedings shall before that time be instituted by other parties."

Those fifteen years were up in 1898. Business had been good for the NYP&N, but the railroad had never gotten quite as much business as expected from Richmond and railroads farther south, and while the NYP&N had brought the PRR system considerable traffic, it had still fallen short paying the interest due on its bonds. The NYP&N was therefore facing a reorganization forced by the PRR. And Cassatt was facing one of the significant challenges of his career. The note recorded in the NYP&N board meeting minutes on the occasion of Cassatt's death praising his dedication to the railroad stated, "At no other time was this more particularly evidenced than during the uncertain period of 1898, when the reorganization of the company became necessary, and to his guiding mind is entirely due the credit for the unprecedented success with which this was accomplished."

The typical nineteenth-century railroad reorganization occurred when a railroad for whatever reason failed to pay interest on its obligations to its bondholders or other creditors. If they demanded payment, they forced the railroad into a state of insolvency, which was technically different from a state of bankruptcy. The reorganization itself was essentially a distribution of losses among the railroad's bondholders, stockholders and any syndicate involved. Needless to say, none of these groups ever wanted to take the biggest hit. When all the interested parties failed to agree, the process required a referee. A court could appoint a receiver, an impartial person who would take custody of the railroad's property and operate the line while its financial organization was being overhauled.

Eventually, the railroad's interested parties would come up with some sort of compromise to cover the railroad's debt and give it sufficient capital to keep running. Existing bonds and shares of stock would be traded for new ones, ideally with as little as possible reduction in value. Usually, the railroad would first meet its obligations to the people it had borrowed money from, with senior bondholders suffering less than junior bondholders and the stockholders with relatively little say in the matter.

In January 1898, Alexander J. Cassatt was already in correspondence with John G. Johnson of 1001 Chestnut Street in Philadelphia, a prominent attorney considered to be one of the best corporate lawyers in the nation.

In a letter dated January 12, 1898, housed with the NYP&N board files at Hagley Museum and Library, Johnson advised Cassatt to allow the Pennsy to formally demand payment on the overdue NYP&N coupons they held. The demand would take six months to mature, allowing time for a reorganization plan to be drafted that would be acceptable to the Pennsy but not look like an attempt to force other bondholders into a deal they were unwilling to enter. Johnson added, "I see no reason why a receivership should be asked for."

At a special meeting of the NYP&N board of directors held on January 24, 1898, the directors acknowledged that it owed PRR and PWB a total of $1,005,330, which it could not pay. The group also needed cash for improvements to the railroad. It therefore resolved to satisfy its existing mortgage obligations and secure a new mortgage to cover all of the railroad's property and equipment and to call in and reissue all of its capital stock.

The Pennsy's board of directors made its official demand for payment on February 9, 1898, noting that the NYP&N owed the Pennsy $486,251.91 and the PWB $519,084.09, which would be payable on September 26, 1898. Cassatt acknowledged that formal notification had been received.

In short order, the NYP&N formed a reorganization committee of three persons, none of them named Cassatt: Rudulph Ellis, Henry W. Biddle and John Lloyd. All three were known in Pennsylvania as financiers, and Ellis was president of the Fidelity Trust Company. By April 2, newspapers were announcing that the committee had a plan requiring a foreclosure and the formation of a new corporation. The committee drafted a plan giving NYP&N bondholders and stockholders the details. It acknowledged that PRR and PWB had been purchasing coupons of the railroad's first lien 6 percent bonds since 1883. Since the NYP&N could not meet its demands for payment, new first mortgage bonds would be issued with the interest reduced from 6 percent to 4 percent, but the holders of these bonds would be issued 10 percent additional bonds. Income bonds would also be reissued with the interest rate reduced from 6 percent to 4 percent, and these bondholders would be assessed 35 percent of the value of their bonds. All stockholders would be assessed 15 percent. The cash generated by the assessments would settle the railroad's debts, build a new steamer and provide funds for terminal facilities in Norfolk. An underwriting syndicate would purchase all first mortgage bonds of people who did not want to participate at par value plus accrued interest. All stock- and bondholders were requested to turn in their securities that summer. The committee assured investors that the new bonds would be a safe and sound investment.

By the end of May, the *Railroad Gazette* reported that two-thirds of NYP&N bondholders had agreed to the reorganization plan, though there were a few discontented dissenters. Some of them united and got a lawyer, whose letter to Cassatt, dated May 3, 1898, is housed in the NYP&N board files at Hagley Museum and Library. The lawyer admonished Cassatt, saying, "You will pardon me for saying that the scheme of reorganization appears to me to be pretty severe on the Income bondholders, and very little time is allowed them for looking about and consulting, and attempting if they so decide to procure some modification of the scheme." Follow-up letters from one of the protesters accused the reorganization committee of failing to provide the bondholders with proper information, implying that the committee's view of the railroad's financial situation did not tally with reports they had previously received. In other words, the NYP&N had done too well for the "junior" bondholders to be assessed 35 percent. By September, their lawyer informed them that while they could contest the reorganization in court, they would be well advised to avoid such tedious and costly litigation and simply get what they could for their bonds.

Early in 1899, the NYP&N stockholders met at the railroad's headquarters in Cape Charles City to put reorganization plans into effect. They also agreed that stocks would be called in and reissued at a lower par value. Although stock would be assessed at 15 percent, the stockholders would receive double the number of shares they had, so their loss would not be as drastic as it seemed. The NYP&N board would also retain some shares of new stock to be issued later.

That March at a board meeting, the PRR board deemed the NYP&N reorganization plan acceptable, providing that the Pennsy got all NYP&N traffic, plus an option to purchase all its stock at any time during the following twenty years that the directors thought they needed to protect their interests.

Following a few weeks spent tracking down individuals who owned an outstanding bond or two, the NYP&N reported on March 28, 1899, that all of its old bonds had been turned in and destroyed. The NYP&N had a new mortgage of $4 million on all of its property with the Fidelity Insurance Trust and Safe Deposit Company of Philadelphia. The reorganization left PRR and PWB owning fewer of NYP&N's securities, but the PRR had the option of taking over the railroad at any time through the time-honored method of stock acquisition.

By June 1899, there were some major changes in the board members and management team of the newly reorganized NYP&N. Pretty much since the railroad's inception, its board had been dominated by Alexander

J. Cassatt, William L. Scott, Cassatt's brother J. Gardner Cassatt, Scott's son-in-law Richard H. Townsend, Uriah Hunt Painter, William A. Patton and Clement A. Griscom, with Cassatt as president and his longtime friend and supporter Patton as vice president. There had been a change in the board's composition in 1892, when John Keller, the contractor who built the railroad, was elected to the board following the death of William L. Scott.

The big news that June was that Alexander J. Cassatt was resigning. He had accepted a much better offer. Cassatt was moving on to become president of the Pennsylvania Railroad Company. In its editorial published June 10, 1899, the *Philadelphia Inquirer* made clear how big of a deal this was: "Seldom has it devolved upon the directors of the Pennsylvania Railroad Company to elect a new president of that corporation. Since its creation only five men have been called to that high position, which is one of the greatest private and quasi-public trusts in the United States, involving as it does the care of properties represented by stocks and bonds amounting to $900,000,000, securities which are not only held by investors in this country, but throughout the world." The editorial continued to endorse Cassatt as the best man for the job, emphasizing his long association with the Pennsy, notwithstanding his leadership of the allied NYP&N: "Since the fall of 1883 he has been one of its [PRR's] directors and for nearly fourteen years he was in close touch with President George B. Roberts, acting as his confidential advisor and keeping thoroughly posted about the broad principles which controlled the conduct of the road."

Following his elevation, Cassatt remained president of the Norfolk and Portsmouth Belt Line Railroad until January 1900, and he did not entirely sever his connection with the NYP&N. On November 15, 1899, the *Virginian Pilot* reported that Cassatt had led a large party of PRR directors and officers to Norfolk via the NYP&N. On the way, they inspected the PRR's newly acquired Baltimore, Chesapeake & Atlantic Railway. They toured the Norfolk harbor and rode the beltline. The paper reported, "The visitors expressed themselves as much gratified with the great progress everywhere visible." Cassatt was also on hand that December in Chester, Pennsylvania, when the NYP&N's fast new passenger steamer, called the *Pennsylvania*, was launched. And throughout the early 1900s, the NYP&N board meetings were often held at PRR's headquarters in its Broad Street Station building in Philadelphia with Cassatt in attendance.

Replacing Alexander J. Cassatt as president was the man who had served as the railroad's vice president since 1884, William A. Patton, who also became president of the Norfolk and Portsmouth Belt Line Railroad after Cassatt

William A. Patton became NYP&N president in 1899. *From* History of the Pennsylvania Railroad, *by William Bender Wilson, 1899.*

resigned that position. Patton had been born in 1849 in a town called Union Furnace in Huntington County, Pennsylvania. He began working for the Pennsy in Altoona in 1865 as a boy in the general superintendent's office but was soon promoted to the more dignified position of clerk. He moved to Philadelphia in 1871 and became chief clerk for Alexander J. Cassatt the following year. When Cassatt officially resigned from the PRR, Patton moved to the PRR president's department, and most recently, he had served as a special assistant in the short-lived administration of PRR president Frank Thomson.

The Historical Society of Pennsylvania houses a scrapbook of congratulatory letters sent to Patton on his promotion written by prominent Pennsylvania businessmen, state officials, politicians and those heading up businesses associated with the NYP&N, such as hotel owners in Old Point Comfort, not to mention individuals brazenly looking for a job. Uriah Hunt Painter, Patton's longtime fellow NYP&N board member, wrote, "Whatever you or Mr. Cassatt see I can do to make this administration a success, let me know....There is much to be done by men, not by 'knaves without brains.'" A letter on PRR stationery from a W.H. Simms, a PRR executive and the stationmaster at PRR's Philadelphia Broad Street Station, alluded to Patton's popularity: "Thousands of the rank and file feel that you deserve the best that life can offer." The same letter also acknowledged Patton's contribution to Cassatt's career: "No one could intelligently estimate how largely you have contributed to Mr. Cassatt's success."

As PRR president, Alexander J. Cassatt is known for his program of sweeping changes and improvements designed to position the Pennsy to handle the demands he envisioned the twentieth century would bring. He began by standardizing shipping rates, thus eliminating the large rebates demanded by major shippers. Probably the most famous and enduring of his many railroad building projects were the twin tunnels beneath the Hudson River that made it possible for Pennsy passengers and their baggage to be carried directly into Manhattan, where they arrived at the new and magnificent Pennsylvania Station.

Throughout the 1880s and 1890s, NYP&N management had been adding to its rolling and floating stock, as well as making relatively modest changes and improvements to the Eastern Shore physical plant on an as-needed basis. In 1890, the board voted in favor of new sidings at Cape Charles City and Delmar and improvements to the railroad's Crisfield branch. When the frame engine house at Cape Charles City burned to the ground in April 1899, the railroad contracted for a new building.

Following the NYP&N's 1899 reorganization and his elevation to PRR president, Cassatt saw to it that the NYP&N had its own more ambitious Eastern Shore improvement and modernization plan. The first major project was the construction of a steel drawbridge over the Pocomoke River replacing the old wooden trestle bridge erected in 1884. The railroad's annual report for 1899 mentioned that not only had this "unsightly structure" been removed, "but an additional element of safety is secured for the increasingly heavy equipment which we are called upon to handle."

In 1900, when the fast new steamer *Pennsylvania* joined existing steamers called the *New York* and the *Old Point Comfort* on voyages between Cape Charles City and Norfolk, the NYP&N's rolling stock included eighteen locomotives, eight passenger coaches and 585 boxcars. At the end of 1902 and the beginning of 1903, Cassatt approached the PRR legal department for advice on how to increase the NYP&N's capital stock to build better terminal facilities and add still more rolling stock and floating equipment. Since this would require a vote from the stockholders, the NYP&N board consequently called a special meeting of shareholders to be held February 10, 1903, at Cape Charles City. Unsurprisingly, they declared the necessity for an additional issue of 5,712½ shares of NYP&N capital stock. The resolution included the proviso "that the holders of the Company's outstanding capital stock shall be accorded the right and privilege of subscribing, in proportion to their respective holdings, for shares of the additional issue at such price not less than par" (or fifty dollars a share).

On June 8, 1906, the *Railroad Gazette* published an article titled "Car Ferry Lines of American Railroads," which featured NYP&N. By that time, NYP&N was operating one wooden car float and five steel car floats, which had quarters amidships for a crew of six. The article noted that NYP&N had begun migrating to steel car floats several years earlier. The improved steel floats had produced "excellent results," and each one had an estimated life of twenty-five years.

The NYP&N had begun dredging and deepening the Cape Charles harbor in 1902, and the new influx of capital led to a major overhaul of

During the day, the bridge over the Pocomoke River remains open for boats. *Author's collection.*

the Cape Charles terminal facilities. In 1904, the railroad purchased 170 acres of land from the Scott estate, extending its property to the south side of the harbor. The same year, NYP&N built an electric light plant to electrify its offices, shops and yards. The 1905 annual report commented that the electric lights were much better than old-fashioned oil lamps for night work. Over the next several years, the railroad built new shops and offices and relocated its roundhouse and car repair shops south of the terminal's main tracks.

Between roughly 1902 and 1905, the railroad began replacing its old sixty-pound rails with eighty-pound steel rails, recycling the old rails for longer sidings to make it easier for lengthy freight trains to pass one another. The ultimate goal was to double track the entire system. In 1908, the NYP&N installed a block signal system for greater speed and safety.

Delmarva residents had long become used to the fact that the place that had been named Cape Charles City had not been located at the geographical Cape Charles, which was the southernmost tip of the peninsula. In 1906, NYP&N announced plans to extend the railroad south to a place known as Kiptopeke, where the ferry trip to Norfolk would be much shorter, and

Cape Charles terminal, circa 1906, where steam-powered vessels could take on coal. *Cape Charles Historical Society, Photograph Collection.*

the local truck farmers would have rail service for the first time. The work was completed by a subsidiary called the Cape Charles Railroad Company (CCRR) in 1912.

Every contemporary railroad had its accidents, often tragic ones. The busier the railroad and the more populated the geography its tracks traversed, the more accidents there were. NYP&N was no exception, and local Delmarva newspapers dutifully reported on every one. Often accidents involved persons or farm animals caught on the tracks, but the more dramatic ones occurred when trains hit other trains, mainly victimizing railroad crew members. On September 24, 1904, the *Harrisburg Patriot* reported that a northbound NYP&N passenger train had collided with a southbound freight at Bloxom, demolishing both engines, killing one fireman and one engineer and severely wounding another engineer. In 1906, the same paper told how a southbound passenger express had run into a southbound freight at Exmore when heavy fog obscured the freight's rear lights. Another engineer died, and his fireman was crushed so badly that he was not expected to recover. The NYP&N's most famous early wreck occurred at Eastville in 1902, when another passenger train collided with a freight. A musical comedy troupe called the Florodoro Company happened to be aboard the passenger train, and several members were injured, including the leading man, who was paralyzed from the waist down. The wreck caught fire, and the uninjured actors organized a bucket brigade.

In the case of the NYP&N, accidents were not confined to dry land. Traffic was high in the waters around Norfolk, where vessels sometimes collided. In 1899, the *Charlotte Daily Observer* reported that a steamer on the Old Dominion Line collided with one of NYP&N's barges, knocking two acid tank cars into the water.

The NYP&N had its heroes, like Thomas Disharoon, the bridge tender at the Pocomoke City drawbridge. On November 29, 1904, Disharoon rushed to close the open drawbridge when he heard the whistle of an approaching freight train. The *Philadelphia Inquirer* reported, "Heroically he stood at his post with no possible chance of escape, knowing that even though he succeeded in relocking the rails his body would be ground under the engine." The engine jumped the track but did not land in the river. In 1907, the *Macon Telegraph* described how NYP&N tugboats had rushed to help douse a fire in a livery stable and three adjoining houses in Cape Charles City, probably saving the town from complete destruction.

The Pennsy and the NYP&N both suffered a tragedy in 1906, when Alexander J. Cassatt died from heart disease at 1:00 p.m. on the afternoon of December 28. During the summer, while staying at the Cassatt summer home in Bar Harbor, Maine, Cassatt had contracted whooping cough from one of his grandchildren. On returning home in September, he worked from his house in Haverford but returned to his office in Broad Street Station in early October. That month, he suffered a cold, but he recovered sufficiently to return to work and had been in the office as recently as December 8. On December 28, he succumbed to a heart attack while seated in a chair at home and died before his physician arrived.

In 1906, the net earnings (gross earnings minus expenses) of the NYP&N were $839,592.19. The railroad carried an average of 360 loaded freight cars a day. It handled over 50,000 through passengers and over 330,000 local passengers. The railroad issued its first stock dividend of 2 percent in 1901. In the summer of 1906, the railroad declared a stock dividend of one share for every four shares outstanding. By July 4, 1908, the *Peninsula Express* reported that it had been paying 12 percent dividends "for the last few years" and proclaimed, "The New York, Philadelphia & Norfolk has been one of the best paying railroads in the country." Its investors had done very well.

It was just a little over a month following Cassatt's death that the members of the NYP&N board indicated that the Pennsy planned to exercise an option it had held open since 1899 and take over the NYP&N through stock acquisition, though it would be about a year before the public was so informed. On June 25, 1908, the *Philadelphia Inquirer* published an article titled "Another Railroad Bought by PRR," explaining that the NYP&N had always been essentially a Pennsy feeder that would be operated more economically once it was wholly absorbed by the larger railroad. The *Inquirer* stated, "The [PRR] Board of Directors decided that the stock of the road should be paid for by 4 per cent. forty-year trust certificates, guaranteed principal and interest by the Pennsylvania Railroad Company on the basis of $3,000 of the certificates for each $1,000 par value of said stock." This meant that the stockholders became bondholders and would continue to receive 12 percent dividends on par value for the following forty years. By October 1908, 49.464 shares of capital stock had been transferred to the Pennsylvania Railroad Company.

By November 1908, Cassatt's son Robert K. and his brother, J. Gardner Cassatt, resigned as NYP&N board members. Longtime board members Henry W. Biddle and John Lloyd also resigned. Joining the board were two senior PRR executives, John P. Green and Samuel Rea, who formed a committee of two to rewrite the railroad's bylaws. William A. Patton remained as president.

The *Philadelphia Inquirer*'s article announcing Pennsy's purchase of the NYP&N also explained, "It has been the policy of the Pennsylvania Railroad for several years to absorb all the smaller roads with which it had traffic or lease agreements." On November 2, 1899, the *Inquirer* had reported, "The Pennsylvania Railroad Company, which recently purchased the Baltimore, Chesapeake and Atlantic Railroad, took charge of the latter system at noon today." The NYP&N had obtained some of its stock, and Robert K. Cassatt, Alexander's son, had been appointed assistant to its new president, Samuel M. Provost, a PRR executive. On March 19, 1904, the *Philadelphia Inquirer* mentioned that Frank Ehlen, then operating the QARR in receivership, had borrowed $20,000 to keep the railroad running and pay some debts that had fallen due. On April 1, the same paper reported that a Wilmington banker named Henry P. Scott was interested in forming a syndicate to gain control of the QARR "for the purpose of disposing of the property to the Pennsylvania Railroad Company."

Early in 1905, a corporation called the Maryland, Delaware and Virginia Railway (MDV) was formed to acquire the QARR, plus a couple steamer lines, which was the reason that the entity had the word *Virginia* in its name. All of its stock was owned by the Pennsy's Baltimore, Chesapeake & Atlantic Railway. On January 23, 1905, the *Philadelphia Inquirer* announced that the officials of the Queen Anne Railroad would host a "brilliant ball and banquet" at the casino at Love Point as a farewell before the railroad formally passed into the hands of its new Pennsy managers. As a byproduct of its acquisition of first the BC&A and then the MDV, the Pennsylvania Railroad was in control of most of the steamship services on the Chesapeake Bay.

On August 3, 1908, the *Harrisburg Patriot* editorialized, "In numerous ways this railroad [NYP&N] has reached a remarkable state of development, and has made an extraordinary contribution to the prosperity and comfort to the territory it reaches," a tribute to the lower Delmarva transformation that might be said to have started with the nine modest railroad stations it set down, in many cases, in the middle of nowhere. Except for the terminal at Cape Charles City, they all looked alike. The two-story wooden buildings each had a ticket office and waiting room beneath living quarters for the ticket agent. The distinctive sloping roofs with eaves overhanging the platforms were not added until the original stations were replaced within about twenty years of the NYP&N's opening. Regardless of exactly who was responsible for the railroad's straight-line design between Delmar and Cape Charles City, it meant that with the possible exception of New Church and Pocomoke City, none of the evenly placed stations was built in an existing town.

Nevertheless, local residents were clamoring for additional stations as early as 1885. On February 7 of that year, the *Peninsula Enterprise* reported that many residents of upper Accomack County had signed a petition for an NYP&N station at a spot then known as Bloxom's Crossing. The editorial stated, "The railroad authorities cannot refuse their demands for better facilities of transportation." Bloxom became one of eleven stations added before 1900. The station at Melfa was added around 1898 to an existing siding and freight house and quickly became an important shipping point. The NYP&N added five more stations between 1900 and 1910, and soon, the railroad had more stops than most other sections of rail in the PRR system.

The NYP&N stations were often named after local landowners, existing estates or prominent individuals, such as Keller for John Keller and Painter honoring William and Uriah Hunt Painter. As had been the case with PRR stations elsewhere, the stations' names were adopted by the towns

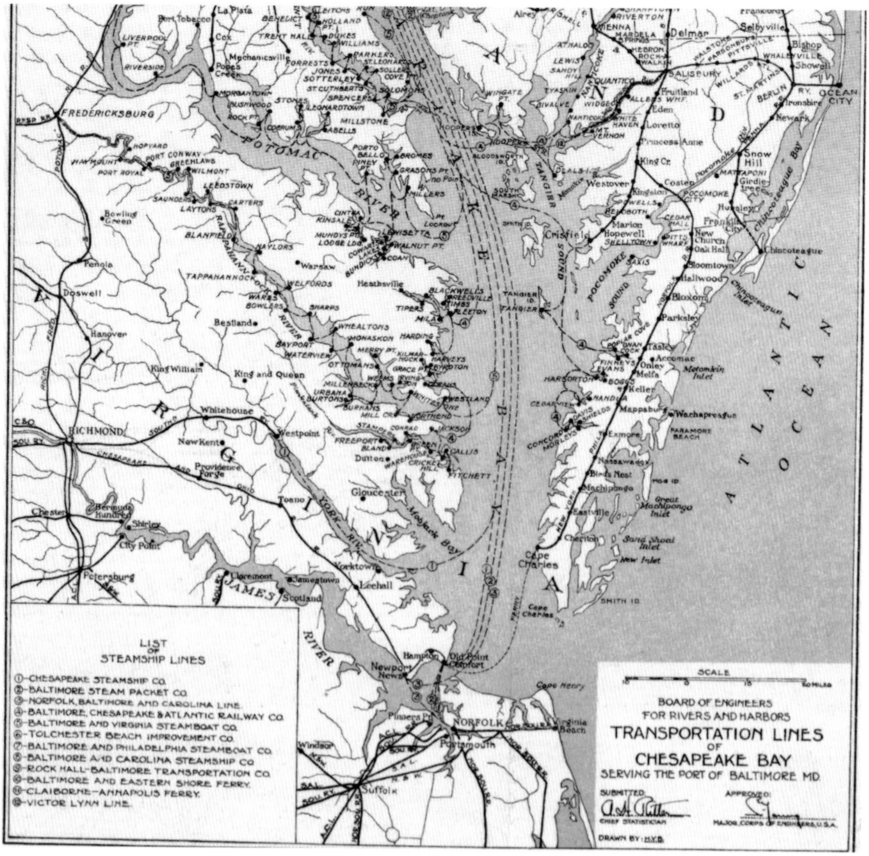

Above: This map, drawn in 1926, shows the NYP&N route through the lower Eastern Shore and its many station stops. *Library of Congress, Geography and Map Division.*

Opposite, top: Bloxom was added as a passenger station before 1900, thanks to local demand for a stop at "Bloxom's Crossing." *Cape Charles Historical Society, Photograph by Ed Sharpe.*

Opposite, bottom: The reconstructed Bloxom passenger station now houses the administrative headquarters of the Cape Charles Historical Society. *Author's collection.*

that grew up around them. Parksley, named after landowner Benjamin Parks, was developed by a traveling salesman from Delaware named Henry R. Bennett, who purchased 160 acres of land and founded the Parksley Land Improvement Company. He laid out a planned community with a commercial district near the railroad tracks. Parallel to the tracks were two avenues named Cassatt Avenue and Patton Avenue. By 1904, when the town incorporated, it had numerous stores, several churches and a hotel. As early as November 1884, the *Baltimore Sun* reported that land near the railroad,

BLOXOM

which had been going for $5 to $10 per acre if purchasers could even be found, was suddenly selling for $20 to $100 per acre.

The peninsula's larger towns were similarly impacted. Pocomoke City attracted mills and factories and became home to many NYP&N employees. Salisbury, the junction of the NYP&N and the BC&A, became a small metropolis and acquired a Union Station, serving both railroads completed in 1914. Crisfield, on the NYP&N branch, continued to develop as a processing center for oysters, clams, crabs and fish.

Besides the railroad's expected positive impact on the trade of Philadelphia to the detriment of Baltimore, the NYP&N impacted other cities on the PRR main line to New York. On July 22, 1887, the *Railroad Gazette* reported that so much "truck" was moving north from North Carolina, Maryland and Virginia that the PRR station facilities in Jersey City had had to be enlarged.

The effects were noted even across the Atlantic. On October 11, 1887, the *Times* in London printed a travel account that reported the same truck farm produce could efficiently reach Boston and even Montreal. The article observed, "A few years ago it [the Eastern Shore] was sparsely peopled by a listless community, whose primitive ways had come down from the last century. Now the farms and forests are changing to fruit and truck gardens, and the stimulus of profitable trade piles up the stations with their produce."

The NYP&N Railroad concurrently brought new influences and commodities to the folks of the Eastern Shore. The advertising pages of the *Peninsula Enterprise* frequently carried an ad for I.H. Merrill & Company, featuring a woodcut illustration of a boxcar with the company's name being drawn south on railroad tracks by a pair of raging bulls. The copy promoted the company's clothing and shoes, promising, "We guarantee to compete with larger cities in styles and prices." In February 1885, the PRR offered special excursion tickets to Eastern Shore farmers who wished to visit Washington for the upcoming presidential inauguration.

The railroad also brought people other than farmers and real estate agents to the Eastern Shore, among them sporting enthusiasts. During the summer of 1885, the *Peninsula Enterprise* mentioned that visitors to Cobbs Island could enjoy bathing, fishing and snipe shooting. Hotels such as the Waddy Hotel in Accomack promised that "hacks" would be on hand to meet the NYP&N trains at their still somewhat isolated stations.

New York sportsmen had once traveled by steamboat to Eastern Shore villages, like Powelton west of the Atlantic Coast barrier islands, to rough it at humble boardinghouses. In 1902, local merchant A.H. Gordon Mears built a thirty-room hotel, which he advertised in northern newspapers and

The tracks of the former NYP&N in Parksley, Virginia. *Author's collection.*

sporting magazines. His carriages met arriving guests at the NYP&N Keller station, and his business boomed. The same year, Powelton was incorporated as Wachapreague, its name supposedly a Native American term meaning "Little City by the Sea." The town soon developed as a resort, also offering a dance hall and poolroom. The hotel continued to welcome guests until it burned down in 1978.

On November 27, 1892, the *New York Times* published an article titled "Mr. Cleveland's Retreat," reporting that Grover Cleveland was vacationing on the Eastern Shore's Hog Island, where he was shooting ducks and snipe. It mentioned that the Old Dominion Club of sportsmen whose clubhouse lay near Wachapreague were planning to send their yacht south to pick him up for a visit. The article also observed, "The main trouble is that the traveling facilities are bringing more sportsmen here all the time, to the disappointment of those who have enjoyed its abundance in the days gone by."

While the NYP&N most dramatically transformed the Delmarva, today's Eastern Shore residents seem to remember most fondly the railroads that took their ancestors to the Atlantic beaches. The Kent Island Heritage Society maintains a railroad station in Stevensville, which has been relocated to what the locals call their town's pocket park behind a popular restaurant. The station, constructed in 1902, would have been the first stop after Love Point on the Queen Anne Railroad to Lewes. It has not been repurposed but rather restored as a historic structure. It houses some furnishings dating from roughly the time it was built. It sits adjacent to a short segment of railroad track supporting a B&O caboose, probably intended as a tribute to the QARR's original Baltimore associations. The station is open to the public but not very often—just the first Saturday of the month during tourist

The remains of the one-thousand-foot pier built by the Baltimore and Eastern Shore Railroad in Claiborne, Maryland. *Author's collection.*

season and on the annual celebration of Kent Island Day. You can also hike part of the QARR right of way, which is now incorporated into the Cross Island Trail through Queen Anne's County, Maryland.

There still exists a genuine, though uncelebrated, artifact of the Delmarva's other trans-peninsula railroad that once took visitors to Ocean City. Drive west of St. Michaels, and you'll find a fork in the road that leads to the present town of Claiborne, which has a number of small cottages below Claiborne Landing, where you can put a boat in the water and park your car and boat trailer. A vintage map indicated that the modern Claiborne Landing was precisely where the B&ES ferries once landed. When we visited on a breezy Wednesday in June 2016, the landing was deserted, and only two cars with boat trailers were parked in its oversized parking spaces. Just beyond the boat ramp, I could see what appeared to be a manmade stretch of land overgrown with trees and foliage that melted into a line of rotting pilings—the remains of the B&ES one-thousand-foot pier.

6

The NYP&N Peaks, Then Begins to Fold in the Twentieth Century

A *Baltimore Sun* article titled "Cape Charles Thrives" published May 2, 1910, hinted that the town's residents felt some apprehension about the fate of their town following Alexander J. Cassatt's death and the Pennsy's takeover of the NYP&N. The article reported, "Persons having investment in Cape Charles until recently looked with suspicion upon the movements of the Pennsylvania Railroad, fearing that at any moment it would change its plans for the future and abandon Cape Charles as a terminus." The locals could witness the construction of the Cape Charles Railroad south of Cape Charles City to Townsend, which would have rail service that December, and then southwest to a new terminus at Kiptopeke, where ferry operations would begin the following year. Apparently, some folks had wondered whether Cape Charles City would become just another depot on the NYP&N main line.

However, the NYP&N's board meeting minutes told a different story. In 1909, the railroad purchased more land in Cape Charles City from the Scott estate for a major enlargement of its classification yards at the edge of the town and the construction of new terminal facilities. The planned project included new offices, large repair facilities, an erecting and machine shop, an engine house, a powerhouse and a seventy-five-foot turntable. All the buildings would be steam heated and electrically lighted. On July 7, 1911, the *Railway Age Gazette* noted, "All locomotive repairs except the heaviest boiler repairs are to be made [in Cape Charles City] now."

A postcard depicting the shops of the NYP&N, circa 1910s. *Cape Charles Historical Society, Photograph Collection.*

A postcard depicting the shops of the NYP&N, circa 1920. *Cape Charles Historical Society, Photograph Collection.*

The new buildings were occupied in 1911 and the railroad's old shops torn down, making more room for freight classification. On March 26, 1911, the *Richmond Times Dispatch* reported that the NYP&N had spent about $500,000 in Cape Charles City the previous year.

The same article mentioned that preparations were then being made for an important part of the project, which would be the construction of a mammoth bridge spanning the rail yards at what had been known as Kellog's Crossing. The bridge would allow both pedestrians and vehicles to cross over the NYP&N yards without having to negotiate their way among moving trains. Nor would their crossing be inconveniently tied up by lengthy, stopped freight trains standing in the way. Construction of the overhead bridge was completed in 1912. The structure became known to the townspeople as the Hump. Although the extensive rail yards and the long freight trains are long gone, crossing the Hump is still the way most folks arrive in Cape Charles City.

In 1913, NYP&N officials met with the town council of Cape Charles, offering to supply the town with the railroad's surplus electric current to light the streets of Cape Charles City.

Before the decade of the 1910s was over, Cape Charles City's harbor was one of the busiest in the nation for its size. The NYP&N employed hundreds of workers in Cape Charles City on round-the-clock shifts. The railroad created even more jobs in its major depot towns of Salisbury, where the NYP&N cooperated with the BC&A on a Union passenger station, and Princess Anne and Crisfield, which both saw major station improvements.

In 1910, on October 2, the *Times Dispatch* reported, "The work of double tracking the New York, Philadelphia and Norfolk Railroad between Delmar

Opposite: A freight train stands in the Cape Charles City rail yard, circa 1915, waiting for its boxcars to be loaded onto car floats. *Cape Charles Historical Society, Photograph Collection.*

Above: Still locally known as the Hump, this 1912 bridge allowed pedestrian and vehicular traffic to safely cross NYP&N tracks. *Cape Charles Historical Society, Photograph Collection.*

and Cape Charles is progressing rapidly." In 1915 and 1916, the railroad's board minutes noted that double-tracking projects had been approved between Hallwood and Parksley and then Parksley to Tasley. Concurrently, the local papers and *Railway Age Gazette* noted astonishing increases in the railroad's rolling stock. In 1913, the railroad's annual report stated that it operated forty locomotives, twenty coaches and over two thousand freight cars. In 1915 and 1916, *Railway Age Gazette* reported that the railroad was purchasing seventy-six ventilated boxcars and six hundred tons of steel for new car floats. During the decade, the NYP&N entered the Pennsy's freight car pool and established a pension system similar to that of the Pennsy.

As the NYP&N grew, so did the town of Cape Charles City. In 1909, the town annexed the land between Pine Street and the shore of the bay, where it constructed two new north–south streets called Bay Street and Harbor Street and extended its existing avenues two blocks west. Known as the Sea Cottage Addition, this became the new fashionable place to build in Cape Charles City. This part of modern Cape Charles City now has some of the Eastern Shore's nicest examples of early twentieth-century domestic architecture, with some of the houses sprawling over double lots.

By 1925, approximately when this photo was taken, Cape Charles City was booming. *Cape Charles Historical Society, Photograph Collection.*

Gentrification apparently brought with it more law-abiding behavior in the once rowdy frontier-like town. By 1920, crime in the town limits was pretty much nonexistent.

Outside the town in the Eastern Shore counties of Virginia, farms grew and farmers prospered, with one crop becoming dominant. On July 3, 1910, the *Richmond Times Dispatch* reported, "Few points in the Unites States excel Cape Charles as a market for sweet and Irish potatoes. The best of market conditions are maintained by buyers, whose alertness and progressiveness, combined with their reliability, give to the grower the 'top of the market,' shipments being made to all territory North and South and as far West as the Rocky Mountains." During what was known as the "trucking season," it was not unusual for over fifteen thousand barrels of potatoes to be handled on Cape Charles City's wharves on a single day. On July 28, 1914, the *Miami Herald* ran an article titled "Farmers Will Get Millions," stating, "The New York, Philadelphia and Norfolk Railroad has been taxed to its utmost to haul these potatoes, and as many as four trains an hour, averaging 50 cars to the train, pass through this city [Cape Charles City] daily bound north."

The NYP&N played an active part in agricultural development. In the early 1910s, the railroad cooperated with the Department of Agriculture in sponsoring a Farmers' Educational Train, which made a multi-day journey throughout Virginia's eastern shore, stopping at various railroad stations where farmers could gather to listen to agricultural experts discourse on topics like soil fertility and pesticides. Locals called the train their "Agricultural College on Wheels." Since the lectures were held right on board the train, farmers attended even in the pouring rain.

In 1916 and 1917, the published annual reports of the NYP&N noted increases in traffic caused by demands on the railroad for foodstuffs and military supplies to support the war then raging in Europe. Revenues were up but so were fuel prices, newly required federal income taxes and labor expenses, thanks to a new law mandating an eight-hour workday. Still, the railroad continued to operate satisfactorily and make improvements to its physical plant.

Not all American railroads were so fortunate. By 1916, a significant percentage were operating in receivership. On December 1, 1917, the Interstate Commerce Commission recommended that President Woodrow Wilson assume control of America's railroads. On December 26, Wilson proclaimed that a government takeover was the only way to ensure efficient railroad operation to mobilize the nation's resources for the war effort.

The resulting legislation, called the Railway Administration Act, became law in March 1918. It stipulated that the takeover was temporary and that the railroads would be returned to their private owners following a peace

In 1925, seasonal workers are arriving by NYP&N steamer to pick strawberries in the rich agricultural Eastern Shore. *Cape Charles Historical Society, Photograph Collection.*

treaty in as good repair as when they were taken over. Wilson appointed William G. McAdoo, then secretary of the treasury, and his son-in-law as director general of railroads.

Among other changes, government-run railroads discouraged civilian passenger travel, resulting in curtailment of any railroad luxury sleeping car service. The government consolidated timetables and ticket offices and centralized the routing of freight. Unlike private railroad management, the goal of the United States Railroad Administration was not making a profit. In the end, the government-operated railroads managed to move troops and war freight, making a significant contribution to the war effort and eventual victory. In 1920, the Esch-Cummins Act returned the nation's railroads to private ownership but also increased the powers of the Interstate Commerce Commission to control their operations.

During the years of government control, the NYP&N continued to publish annual reports, but these did not have much to say because the company's cash balance had been transferred to the United States Railroad Administration. The NYP&N had been assured it would receive "adequate return" for the use of its property, but the feds were not providing operating statistics. The railroad made only those improvements absolutely necessary for safety.

On December 31, 1918, NYP&N's longtime president William A. Patton resigned, citing "impaired health" as the reason. A letter in volume two of the Patton Papers, housed at the Historical Society of Pennsylvania, hints at a different reason. The superintendent of PRR's eastern lines wrote Patton, "The gentle art of railroading has so changed under War conditions that it must be a great relief to be able to leave the present turmoil and reflect upon other—and I am sure I will be pardoned for saying—better days."

The very close association of Patton with Alexander J. Cassatt was noted in the NYP&N board minutes of January 14, 1919. The minutes commented, "His [Patton's] railroad career was closely identified with Mr. Cassatt with whom he stood in the most confidential relation for more than thirty years, so that this company has enjoyed the unusual advantage of his conscientious and intelligent devotion to its interests, coupled with a familiarity with the aims and policies of his illustrious predecessor." To succeed Patton, the board nominated Samuel Rea, who had been president of the Pennsylvania Railroad since 1913.

While the nation's railroads were still under federal control, senior management at the Pennsy was already making plans for more efficient operation and administration of the many railroads in its family through consolidation. As early as the summer of 1917, there were rumors that the NYP&N would be brought into closer association with the Pennsy, and early in 1918, their traffic and operating departments were merged.

The NYP&N was concurrently doing some consolidation of its own. The NYP&N already owned all outstanding capital stock of the Cape Charles Railroad, which had constructed the short line between Cape Charles and Kiptopeke. In November 1917, the NYP&N board ordered all of the CCRR stock to be delivered. The shares were cancelled together with CCRR's debts. Early in 1918, the CCRR as a separate entity was officially dissolved.

On February 11, 1918, the NYP&N board minutes first mentioned that the railroad and all its property and franchises would be leased to the Pennsy "to secure a more economical operation and to more adequately provide for accommodating traffic." On February 25, 1920, with the end of federal control imminent, the NYP&N minutes state that the PRR proposed to operate all of its lines as a single system divided among four regions: Eastern, Central, Northwestern and Southwestern. The NYP&N would henceforward operate in the Norfolk Division of the Pennsy's Eastern Region.

By December 1920, the Pennsy's legal department had drawn up the final lease agreement. The Pennsy would lease the NYP&N, starting December 14, for a period of 999 years. NYP&N stockholders had approved the agreement on June 30, 1920. No shareholders had voted no, but then PRR interests held all of the NYP&N shares. It took a little longer for the Interstate Commerce Commission, but that body also approved the Pennsy's control by lease of the NYP&N on August 11, 1921, opening the way for the actual takeover to become effective in 1922. The *Richmond Times Dispatch* made the public announcement on November 12, 1922: "On November 1, under terms of a 999-year lease, the New York, Philadelphia and Norfolk Railroad formally passed into the possession of the Pennsylvania Railroad Company." The reporter added, "No visible change is brought about, for the line which serves the Eastern Shore of Virginia has been practically a part of the Pennsylvania system for years." What had started in 1881 with the PRR takeover of the Philadelphia, Wilmington and Baltimore Railroad had reached completion; the Pennsy had a rail transportation monopoly on the Delmarva Peninsula.

In early September 1922, several newspapers carried the story of record business on the NYP&N car floats. During the previous month, a total of 27,943 rail cars had been towed across the bay, representing not only the

This page: Two images of car floats in operation, circa 1920s. *Cape Charles Historical Society, Photograph Collection.*

How boxcars were loaded onto car floats at Cape Charles City, circa 1924. *Cape Charles Historical Society, Photograph Collection.*

heaviest traffic ever for this route, but also possibly the heaviest traffic ever for any car ferry of equal length in the world. By 1924, the railroad had reduced the length of time it took to dock, unload and reload a car float to one hour or less. So began the Roaring Twenties for the railroad and its terminal town.

The NYP&N left behind the days of wartime austerity in passenger travel by placing in operation many fine express and overnight trains with luxury accommodations and fine-dining service. These trains became very popular with travelers who appreciated the efficient and comfortable steamer-rail service between Norfolk and the Northeast. In 1928, the NYP&N's most fondly remembered steamer, the *Virginia Lee*, went into service. The ship could transport up to 1,200 passengers and offered the luxury of private cabins.

During the 1920s, the Eastern Shore island community of Chincoteague finally got access to NYP&N rail service. Chincoteague had long enjoyed a profitable seafood industry but had previously shipped out all of its oysters, clams and fish by boat. In 1922, island residents finally constructed a road over the marshes and salt flats that separated it from the mainland and established a connection with the NYP&N at Lecato, allowing them to ship out seafood faster and fresher.

In the same 1922 article in which the *Richmond Times Dispatch* announced the NYP&N's lease to the Pennsy, NYP&N vice president Elisha Lee was

This page and opposite: Images of steamers docking at Cape Charles City, also showing the development of the terminal and docking facilities. *Cape Charles Historical Society, Photograph Collection.*

reported as saying, "The railroad has purchased 1,000 acres of land and necessary water rights at the mouth of Little Creek [on the western shore]. In the not distant future barges carrying laden freight cars will ply between that point and Cape Charles." Funds had been appropriated for a new NYP&N Western Shore terminal in June 1917, but the project had been postponed during the federal takeover of railroads by the United States Railroad Administration. Establishing a terminal at Little Creek near what is now Virginia Beach would allow for larger terminal facilities, shorten the

An elegant dining room aboard the steamer *Elisha Lee* in 1944. *Cape Charles Historical Society, Photograph Collection.*

water route from thirty-six miles to twenty-seven and avoid the increasingly congested Norfolk Harbor and Elizabeth River. It would also allow the NYP&N to connect directly with Norfolk Southern Railroad and other lines south without having to connect via the beltline.

In 1924, the NYP&N board minutes estimated the cost of the project at $2,611,138. On January 22, 1930, the minutes reported that the project had actually cost $3,100,000, but other historians have estimated the real cost closer to $5,000,000.

Construction began in December 1926, following the inevitable delay in waiting for ICC approval. In 1927 and 1928, the NYP&N stated in its annual reports that construction was progressing, and the railroad was making the necessary arrangements with Norfolk Southern. The new Little Creek terminal opened on January 3, 1929, with the superintendent of PRR's Norfolk Division on hand to witness the first car float arrive. The Pennsy hoped that the project would soon pay off by placing the railroad in position for much expected future growth.

This Baldwin locomotive was photographed in 1935 at Little Creek, Virginia, where NYP&N built an expanded terminal in the 1920s. *Cape Charles Historical Society, Photograph by Ed Sharpe.*

About a year after the stock market crash of 1929, when it had become clear to both politicians and businessmen that the U.S. economy was in a depression, those residing at both ends of the NYP&N ferry route hoped that their state-of-the-art transportation system would help their region escape the economic downturn. At PRR's Philadelphia headquarters, Pennsy management responded to the threat with further consolidation, combining its Norfolk and Delaware Divisions into a single Delmarva Division, including all lines on the peninsula south of Porter, Delaware, as well as the Cape Charles to Norfolk ferry. The rest of the former Delaware Division between Porter and Wilmington would become part of PRR's Maryland Division.

During the rest of the decade, the Pennsy discovered that it also needed to downsize to reflect its Depression-incurred loss of traffic. The NYP&N's annual reports for the decade recorded the sale and/or retirement of buildings, equipment, platforms, locomotives, freight cars and car floats. The NYP&N also reduced its footprint on land, granting property on the south side of Little Creek to the federal government for a Coast Guard station and selling land to the town of Cape Charles City for a bulkhead that the town would maintain for small watercraft. PRR curtailed its passenger steamboat operations throughout the Chesapeake Bay.

A newspaper account of a tragic rail accident on the NYP&N route also showed how Americans could rally when dealing with adversity. Written by

John Kieran for the sports pages of the *New York Times* and published on April 6, 1933, with the headline "Off the Rails with the Red Sox," it told the story of what was perhaps the most famous train wreck in this railroad's history. The Boston Red Sox were on their way north from Florida on NYP&N's passenger express, called the Cavalier, when the train's locomotive and eight of its twelve cars crashed through an open switch that PRR later suspected had been tampered with. The train had been traveling about fifty miles per hour, and its engineer and fireman were both killed.

The Red Sox ballplayers had been asleep when the accident occurred at 3:15 a.m., about five miles south of Dover. Uninjured in their Pullman car, they looked out the windows to find themselves in a cornfield. They dressed quickly and rushed out to aid passengers in the coaches between the Pullman cars and the baggage cars. Once the players hauled out the injured, the team doctor patched them up with his first aid kit. Other athletes investigated a trackside canning factory where the baggage cars had plowed through its wall but were reassured by the factory's night watchman that what they saw on the floor was spilled canned tomatoes and not blood. While waiting for a rescue train to take them north, the athletes retrieved their trunks and equipment from the wrecked baggage cars and were amazed to discover that their balls and bats had escaped so much as a scratch. The article's author reported, "They climbed aboard the rescue train and went off to defeat Jersey City that afternoon as though nothing had happened." Kieran quoted the team's manager Marty McManus: "That's a warning to the other clubs in the league....We're tough this year."

The prosperity of the 1920s was not shared equally by all rail lines on the Delmarva Peninsula. The Maryland, Delaware and Virginia Railway was consistently operating in the red since 1911 but stayed in business because the Baltimore, Chesapeake & Atlantic Railway had guaranteed the interest on its bonds. By 1923, the MDV had become enough of a burden on the Pennsy to be allowed to enter bankruptcy and be sold at foreclosure. The PRR then formed the Baltimore and Virginia Steamboat Company to pick up some of its steamer lines but simply dropped others. Similarly, some MDV rail lines were scrapped while others became part of another new company called the Baltimore and Eastern Railroad, a subsidiary of the Pennsy's BC&A. The Baltimore and Eastern began operations in 1924, continuing to carry passengers to Ocean City with locomotives rented from the BC&A.

However, during the 1920s, business was not so good for the BC&A either. From the late 1910s to the mid-1920s, it racked up deficits that grew every year, until the Pennsy also forced it into bankruptcy in 1926. It was sold in March 1928. The Baltimore and Virginia Steamboat Company picked up most of its steamer operations while the BC&A's former subsidiary, the Baltimore and Eastern, purchased some of its rail operations, plus its ferry between Baltimore and Claiborne, Maryland.

During the 1930s, the PRR curtailed service on portions of the B&E that proved to be increasingly unprofitable and did little to maintain the railroad's infrastructure. In 1938, the B&E filed a petition with the Interstate Commerce Commission, seeking to abandon some of the remaining segments of its lines, including the rails between West Ocean City and Ocean City. What had been intended as a trunk line and had operated as a beloved route to an ocean resort became a dismembered collection of short lines.

It wasn't that people stopped wanting to visit nice places like the seashore, even during hard times, but the first four decades of the twentieth century brought the traveling public an alternative to trains. In the early years of the twentieth century, the few fortunate folks who owned motor cars joined motor clubs, mainly so they could share information on the best way of getting places on the nation's roads, which by no means had yet formed a network of highways.

On April 27, 1907, the *Harrisburg Patriot* published advice for those autoists planning to visit the Jamestown Exposition that summer. It came from a member of a New York auto club who had come to address the Motor Club of Harrisburg about the 240-mile route he had explored. He advised the Harrisburg motorists to drive to Philadelphia, where they could proceed south through Wilmington and Dover. The New York motorist, a Mr. R.H. Johnston, reported, "The sand roads south of Wilmington are relieved at intervals by stretches of magnificent shell roads, which are simply ideal from this motorist's point of view." However, the roads around Norfolk were "very poor," so Harrisburg travelers were advised to leave their cars in Cape Charles City, take the NYP&N ferry across the bay to Old Point Comfort and then use local ferries to get to the exposition and other points of interest. The trip to Cape Charles City would take three days, and the best towns for overnight stays were Dover and Princess Anne.

The American auto clubs were also instrumental in petitioning state and local governments to make the roads safer and better suited for automobile travel. By 1924, Delaware had a north–south highway running through most of the state. A 1921 article in the *Lexington* [Kentucky] *Herald* reported that Maryland had a hard surfaced road running south from Elkton lined with telegraph poles and trees that had been whitewashed up to a height of four feet so that motorists could find the road at night. The conditions

A view of the NYP&N terminal, circa 1925, as automobiles were becoming increasingly popular. *Cape Charles Historical Society, Photograph Collection.*

in Eastern Shore Virginia, where the roads had until lately been dusty and thick with encroaching foliage, improved in 1923, with construction of what is now U.S. Highway 13 starting north from the town of Cape Charles City. By 1931, motorists could find a continuous ribbon of concrete between the geographical Cape Charles and the Maryland-Virginia line, which widened here and there to three and even four lanes.

On August 18, 1930, the *New York Times* announced that the Pennsylvania Railroad planned to offer passengers bus service between Norfolk and New York via Wilmington and Philadelphia through its subsidiary the Pennsylvania-Virginia General Transit Company. Between Cape Charles City and Norfolk, passengers would take the railroad's ferry. Even those who could not afford their own automobile then had an alternative to the train.

The improving roads of the 1920s called attention to the fact that the NYP&N's passenger ferries had not been designed to carry automobiles. And unlike those visiting the Jamestown Exposition of 1907, the motorists of the 1920s were not content to leave their cars in Cape Charles City. They wanted to take their cars with them to explore Virginia or drive farther south. In the early 1920s, the railroad began to handle automobiles on the passenger ferries but treated them as cumbersome freight. Their gas tanks had to be emptied to comply with contemporary fire regulations, which then made it necessary for dock workers to push the cars on and off the steamships, a service for which the railroad's charges were discouragingly high. By the middle of the decade, the railroad had succumbed to consumer demand by constructing automobile loading ramps on its docks, adapting its steamships to allow room for motor cars and reducing charges.

By 1930, the railroad had something to spur it to further accommodation, namely, competition. In July, a Richmond-based business called the Peninsula Ferry Corporation applied to the local circuit court for a franchise to ferry motorists and their cars from Cape Charles City to a point near Norfolk. A judge granted the application, and the Pennsy contested in court but lost.

The Pennsy countered more successfully by forming its own Virginia Ferry Corporation (VFC) in 1933, which promptly absorbed the Peninsula Ferry Company's franchise. The NYP&N's board minutes show that the railroad hastened to agree that the new Virginia Ferry Corporation could use the railroad's terminals and dock facilities at both Cape Charles City and Little Creek.

The VFC leased passenger ferries from the railroad while awaiting delivery of its own vessel, the *Delmarva*, which arrived in January 1934. Unlike the earlier passenger steamers, the *Delmarva* had wide doors at both bow and stern, allowing motor vehicles to be driven on and off a special auto deck.

The ease with which motorists could get their cars across the Chesapeake made the Pennsy's Virginia Ferry Corporation a link in what became known as the nation's Ocean Highway, an increasingly popular motor route between New York and Florida, also sometimes called the Pines to Palms Route. On October 11, 1936, in an article titled "Improved Highway to the South," a *New York Times* writer observed, "The [highway's] development embodies recognition of the motorist as a patron who brings trade to the cities and towns through which he passes, and to hotels, restaurants, service stations, amusements, etc. along his way." The author warned travelers to figure the VFC ferry schedule into one's plans but added, "If one misses the last sailing one may put the car aboard and spend the night on the vessel. It has lounges, dining room, game room, and play room for children."

During the same decades in which automobiles became popular with American travelers, more and more of the Delmarva's produce started moving north by truck. On August 12, 1928, the *New York Times* carried an article about Crisfield, Maryland, titled "In the Busy Crab Capital of America" by Gertrude Shelby. Shelby wrote, "Every night but Saturday a whole fleet of trucks rush breakneck out of Crisfield, bound for Philadelphia,

New York and Boston—principally New York." By the 1930s, with improved highways, most of Delmarva's perishable agricultural products were being shipped out by motor carriers.

The Pennsy's loss of passenger and freight business was briefly reversed by World War II, when railroads once again proved to be the most efficient way of transporting war materials and military personnel. Because there were a great many military bases in and around Hampton Roads, this meant a dramatic increase in business for the Pennsy, and in particular, its NYP&N route. The tracks and ferries handled coal trains and troop trains. For the sake of military personnel stationed in the Norfolk area, every Sunday, the PRR operated a special train from New York to Cape Charles City called the Furlough, which met a special ferry that got the men back to their bases from weekend leave. The Pennsy also temporarily withdrew its sleeping cars from many routes, including New York to Norfolk, so that the cars could be converted for military needs in accordance with orders from the Office of Defense Transportation.

After the war was over, Americans weary of gasoline and tire rationing, as well as mainland travel restrictions, were happy to get back in their cars and drive. In a *New York Times* article published February 29, 1948, titled "Short Trips South," author Crerar Harris doled out advice for New Yorkers sick of winter weather: "The quickest and easiest way to get out of the snow belt, is to head for Cape Charles, Va., a convenient gateway to all southern points, at the tip of the fascinating Delmarva peninsula." Unlike the earlier years of the century, a driver could leave New York City in the morning and be in Cape Charles City by dinnertime. Government-subsidized highways would shortly make motor trips even more convenient.

To make things easier for drivers, the Virginia Ferry Corporation announced in 1948 that it would move its Eastern Shore ferry terminal from Cape Charles City to what would become the town of Kiptopeke, which was farther south and would shave about half an hour off the bay crossing. On January 22, 1950, the *New York Times* reported that Kiptopeke's new ferry terminal had been constructed and "plans are under way for a large hotel of advanced design, a terminal building and motor court." By June 8, 1952, the *Times* published an article titled "Chesapeake Crossing," in which author Frances W. Brown advised motorists that crossing the bay at Kiptopeke was superior to the ferries that still ran from Cape Charles City: "Catching the ferry at Kiptopeke Beach is not the life-or-death matter that it is at Cape Charles, for these fast, modern, radar-equipped boats run on an approximately hourly schedule from 3 A.M. till midnight."

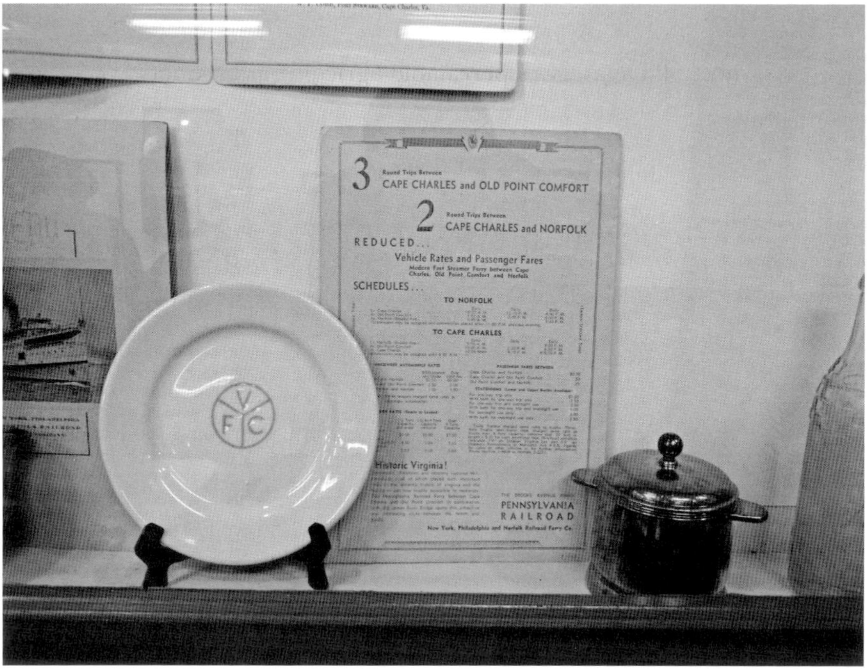

Artifacts of ferry crossings housed at the Eastern Shore Railway Museum. *Author's collection.*

Its loss of passenger traffic to automobiles and freight to trucks apparently caused the postwar Pennsy to downgrade the old NYP&N route as a trunk line and through route during the early 1950s. However, the railroad made no such announcement, and when workmen began removing the NYP&N's second track between Cape Charles City and Pocomoke City in 1954, the railroad cited as the reason the improved efficiency it expected from its new diesel locomotives, but the railroad did little to maintain its remaining Delmarva tracks or promote business on the NYP&N route.

In 1955, the Pennsylvania Railroad consolidated nineteen divisions into nine regions, placing the former PRR Delmarva Division into its new Chesapeake Region, whose headquarters would be in Philadelphia, not Cape Charles City. During the 1950s, the Pennsy further reduced its Eastern Shore presence by closing its office in Princess Anne; selling to the town of Crisfield its wharf, freight shed, office and platforms over the Annemessix River; and abandoning all facilities it still operated at Port Norfolk, including tracks, warehouses and transfer bridges.

In 1950, the Pennsy closed six Eastern Shore passenger stations and began dropping passenger trains from service on the NYP&N route. By

1956, it was down to one passenger train per day, called the Delmarva Express, which the railroad kept running mainly because it had a contract to deliver the U.S. mail.

On November 1, 1957, the *New York Times* reported that the Pennsylvania Railroad had applied to Maryland and Virginia public utility commissions for permission to discontinue all passenger service between Delmar and Cape Charles City. On January 11, 1958, the Delmarva Express pulled out of Cape Charles City for the last time.

Since only diesel freight trains would be arriving and departing from Cape Charles City, there was no need for the Pennsy to maintain useless empty buildings there. Demolition began with the old NYP&N terminal building in 1959. By 1961, PRR had demolished most of its Cape Charles City facilities, including its shops and engine house.

During the 1950s, the Pennsy was also working on abandoning its passenger ferry service out of Cape Charles City. Its steamer, called the *Maryland*, was sold for scrap in 1950. Its fondly recalled flagship, the *Virginia Lee*, had been requisitioned by the government for wartime use in 1942 and had never been returned to its original route. PRR's remaining steamer, the *Elisha Lee*, cost a lot of money to be maintained to Coast Guard standards, prompting the railroad to petition a Virginia judge to suspend ferry service and surrender its franchise in 1953. Although the court ordered the Pennsy to continue service for thirty days pending further hearings, the railroad chose instead to pay a fine for contempt. The *Elisha Lee* made its final run across the Chesapeake on February 28. On March 1, the *Elisha Lee* failed a Coast Guard inspection, and the Pennsy sold it for scrap rather than spend the cash to fix it. Official permission to abandon passenger ferry service came from the ICC in mid-1954, and the official liquidation occurred in the fall of 1955, when the railroad sold its remaining ferry property and facilities to the Chesapeake Bay Ferry District to cover its debts.

In 1956, the public agency called the Chesapeake Bay Ferry Commission, which operated the entity called the Chesapeake Bay Ferry District, also purchased the operations of the Virginia Ferry Corporation that had been transporting passengers and automobiles from Kiptopeke to Little Creek. A $20 million bond issue had financed the acquisition. Newspaper articles announcing this deal also happened to mention that the commission was studying the feasibility of replacing all ferry operations with some sort of causeway across the bay, which might consist of a bridge, a tunnel or both. The commission had been authorized to spend $500,000 for a survey.

7

Picking Up the Pieces of the NYP&N

The earliest documentary evidence of the concept of bridging the Chesapeake Bay can be found in the 1926 board files of the Baltimore, Chesapeake & Atlantic Railway. The contemplated bridge would have stretched between Bay Shore Resort near Baltimore to a point near the town of Rock Hall. The Baltimore Association of Commerce endorsed the idea. The BC&A considered a prospectus, but the railroad's president rejected it because it did not stand to earn much money for the railroad. Other factors might have included the bankruptcy the BC&A was facing and the possible opposition from its controlling authority, the Pennsylvania Railroad.

The next call for a bridge across the Chesapeake came in 1938 from Maryland's general assembly. The proposed location was Sandy Point near Annapolis on the western shore to Kent Island. Authorizing legislation passed, but World War II got in the way. Finally, in 1947, the assembly, led by Maryland's governor William Preston Lane Jr., passed legislation directing construction to begin. On January 12, 1949, Lane met with officials at Sandy Point to get the project underway. In his address that day, the governor mentioned that the bridge would be financed with bonds and tolls. Its estimated cost at the time was $44 million.

This made the Chesapeake Bay Bridge a much bigger project than another bridge construction project underway farther north in the state. In 1942, a tanker had knocked down the drawbridge spanning the Chesapeake and Delaware Canal at Chesapeake City. Because it was wartime, the bridge was replaced by ferry service until 1949, when $4 million was spent on a new bridge long enough and high enough to keep traffic moving both north and south on Route 213 and east and west on the canal without the need for bridge openings.

While the Chesapeake Bay Bridge was under construction, so was a massive highway improvement project intended to bring the roads of Maryland's Eastern Shore up to date. Once across the bridge, motorists heading east would be on an expressway that would branch north to connect with the highway system of Delaware or south to Ocean City. The larger idea was to create an alternate route between Wilmington and Washington, D.C., and to mimic the old route of the BC&A, giving residents of Baltimore and Washington easy access to Ocean City.

Officially named the William Preston Lane Jr. Memorial Bridge, the Chesapeake Bay span opened for traffic on July 30, 1952. At 4.3 miles in length, it was the world's largest steel structure over water. It quickly made Maryland's Queen Anne County a bedroom community for the state capital in Annapolis and eventually Washington, D.C., and contributed to the growth of Ocean City. Improvements were made to both the bridge and its connecting highways through the ensuing years, and by 1973, a second parallel span was added to accommodate traffic.

The Chesapeake Bay Bridge (which people persist in calling it rather than the Lane Memorial Bridge) eliminated the need for state-run ferry service between Sandy Point and Matapeake on Kent Island, which was not far south of the eastern end of the bridge. There was a short-lived effort on the part of folks living farther south on the eastern shore to get the state's ferry service moved to cross the bay from a point on the Potomac River to Crisfield, where two other ferries carried tourists to Smith and Tangier Islands. However, as E. John Long of the *New York Times* reported on March 23, 1952, "It is an open secret that the [Chesapeake Bay Ferry] commission would like to get out of the ferry business and has had several offers to dispose of the boats at a satisfactory price."

In a few more years, the commission was openly looking to get out of the ferry business it had purchased from the Pennsy; however, a bridge across the bay where the NYP&N had run its ferries and car floats would require a structure about eighteen miles long. It would need to rise quite high over the channel, which large merchant ships used to reach Hampton Roads and the ports of Baltimore, Annapolis and Washington, D.C. It would have to be strategically designed so that the navy's Atlantic fleet would not be bottled up in Norfolk if an enemy sought to destroy the structure. Eventually, a design emerged that was called by some the "over-under highway." The new bridge would be a causeway interrupted by a raised span and two tunnels leaving plenty of room for ships to maneuver in and out of the Chesapeake Bay. On September 3, 1956, the *New York Times* reported in a brief news article that the Pennsylvania Railroad was conducting a special study for a "rail adjunct" to the proposed bridge-tunnel at the request of the Chesapeake Bay Ferry Commission, but nothing ever came of this proposal.

In the summer of 1960, the commission sold $200 million in revenue bonds whose interest and principal were intended to be covered by bridge tolls. Contracts were awarded, and construction began that October. During the three and a half years it took to construct the Chesapeake Bay Bridge-Tunnel, hopes rose that the connection would bring growth and business not only to Norfolk and Hampton Roads but also communities as far away as Virginia Beach, Nags Head in North Carolina and Milford in Delaware, not to mention the Virginia towns on the eastern shore. The bridge opened on April 15, 1964, and the American Society of Civil Engineers soon proclaimed it to be one of the seven engineering wonders of the world.

When the bridge-tunnel opened, motorists paid a toll of just fifteen cents more than they had been paying for a ferry ticket. Truckers paid less than the ferry had cost them, and the trip saved all commuters about an hour. During the early years of its operation, the bridge-tunnel's causeway sometimes had to be closed when ships accidentally slammed into it in choppy seas. Although traffic was not quite as heavy as its planners had expected, the bridge-tunnel was sufficiently successful that by 1987, the public agency then called the Chesapeake Bay Bridge and Tunnel Commission was considering a parallel bridge and causeway to meet anticipated future demands. Virginia's general assembly approved the project in 1990, and construction began in 1995. The project did not include parallel tunnels, which continue to be a bottleneck at times. Replacing the two-lane tunnels with deeper, wider, four-lane tunnels remains under consideration.

While the Chesapeake Bay bridges were being envisioned, designed and surveyed, Delmarva's rail service was facing extinction, and it was not entirely the bridges' fault. In 1968, the once formidable Pennsylvania Railroad Company was forced by its financial condition to merge with its archrival, the New York Central Railroad, to form the Penn Central. The new entity regarded the former NYP&N route not as a trunk line but rather an expendable feeder and so allowed track conditions and service to deteriorate. Once the Penn Central was also facing bankruptcy, its plans for many other Delmarva lines involved abandonment rather than repair.

This car float was photographed in 1966 after the Chesapeake Bay Bridge-Tunnel opened, while its effect on NYP&N traffic was still uncertain. *Cape Charles Historical Society, Photograph by Ed Sharpe.*

In 1973, Congress passed legislation to form a government-backed company called the Consolidated Rail Corporation (Conrail) to take over those portions of bankrupt railroads still considered viable. On March 28, 1976, the *New York Times* announced that Conrail "has reached agreements to continue essential rail services on the Delmarva Peninsula, including the car float across the Chesapeake Bay and rail operations in Norfolk, Va."

It soon became clear that Conrail planned to confine service to the tracks between Wilmington and Pocomoke City, with occasional runs to Salisbury and Ocean City. Government officials in Delaware and Maryland made deals with Conrail that would allow local operators to run trains on what Conrail considered money-losing branches with federal subsidies that would be gradually phased out. But by that time, track conditions on the Delmarva Peninsula were so poor that even those trains running on what were the remaining main lines were forced to lumber along at about eight miles per hour, and still, they suffered frequent derailments.

In 1977, Maryland's Department of Transportation selected a newly created operator called the Maryland and Delaware Railroad Company (MDDE) to run trains between Seaford, Delaware, and Cambridge, Maryland; Chestertown and Centreville in Maryland; and Clayton,

The Cape Charles rail and passenger terminal just before the merger of PRR with the New York Central. *Cape Charles Historical Society, Photograph by Ed Sharpe.*

The Cape Charles rail yard in the 1970s, around the time Conrail was formed. *Cape Charles Historical Society, Photograph by Ed Sharpe.*

Delaware, to Easton, Maryland. All three were lines that Conrail had intended to discontinue. By 1980, *New York Times* reporter Ernest Holsendolph was calling the MDDE a success. In a November 2 article titled "How to Survive on the Rails," the author quoted MDDE president J. Anthony Hannold's opinion that "where hard work and caring a lot about service can make a difference, short lines are viable." The president also admitted that having fewer employees who did not earn union wages also contributed to MDDE's viability. From its tiny headquarters in a former train station in Federalsburg, Maryland, the MDDE kept local farmers and businessmen linked with Conrail in the North and Norfolk and Western in the South.

By 1982, MDDE was modestly expanding. A local organization called the Snow Hill Shippers Association had purchased a branch between Frankford, Delaware, and Snow Hill, Maryland, and hired MDDE to run trains, which the railroad did until MDDE itself bought this line in 2000. In 1994, Delaware awarded MDDE a contract to operate between Ellendale and Milton and Georgetown and Lewes, though MDDE decided not to renew the contract in 1999, when these lines reverted to their former operator, called the Delaware Coast Line, which later became part of Delmarva Central Railroad. In 2008, a local paper, the *Chesapeake Business Ledger*, reported that traffic was stable on MDDE's 120 miles of track, keeping locals connected with the rest of the United States via connections with Norfolk Southern.

Today, MDDE operates over much of the same trackage, with three lines that are disconnected with each other but each connected with Norfolk Southern. From an interchange at Townsend, Delaware, MDDE trains run to Massey, where one MDDE line continues to Centreville, and another called the Chestertown Line terminates in Worton. Farther south, MDDE's Seaford Line handles trains running from Seaford through the railroad's headquarters in Federalsburg to Cambridge. MDDE's Snow Hill Line connects with Norfolk Southern in Frankford, Delaware, and runs to Snow Hill.

Each year in October, the town of Hurlock hosts its fall festival, where MDDE cooperates with the town and volunteers to operate two vintage passenger coaches on a popular ride from Hurlock's train station to Federalsburg on MDDE's Seaford Line, a tiny segment remaining of what had been conceived as a trunk line from Baltimore to Ocean City. For many younger Eastern Shore residents, this can be their one and only chance to ride a passenger train. For dedicated railfans, it's a chance to add "rare miles" to their collection of rail experiences. If you just want to see the passenger coaches, they're parked on a siding in a field off Route 307, or Broad Street in Hurlock, near the active MDDE tracks.

Passenger cars owned by the Town of Hurlock, Maryland. *Author's collection.*

On a cloudy spring day in 2014, we left our hotel in St. Michaels for MDDE headquarters in Federalsburg to meet with MDDE president Eric H. Callaway. We crossed the Choptank and traversed a lot of farmland. We found railroad tracks and the train station easily enough when we entered the town. Furnished with about six desks, the tiny railroad station could be described as cozy, and Mr. Callaway was, to say the least, colorful.

He told us he had spent his entire working life with MDDE, starting soon after high school graduation, when he realized that his family's farm was not going to support him and his siblings. The day Callaway hitchhiked to the MDDE office, Mr. Hannold personally hired him to drive in loose spikes along the tracks with a ten-pound maul. Over the decades, he came to run the railroad with two partners. The three owned all of the stock of the railroad, which was structured as a C-corporation. The railroad employed fifteen people, some of them part-timers.

Mr. Callaway told us that business was "steady" and had been for the last thirty years. Besides regularly hauling grain and fertilizer for the local poultry industry, MDDE also carried propane gas in the winter and wheat and soybeans in the fall. He commented, "If the money is right, we'll haul anything."

Headquarters of the modern-day Maryland and Delaware Railroad in Federalsburg, Maryland. *Author's collection.*

He described some abridgement of the MDDE system since the business was created in 1977. The State of Maryland had abandoned the tracks it had owned between Clayton and Easton for lack of business. The state had rebuilt the rail yard in Chestertown, but after a wind shear damaged the tracks there, MDDE abandoned the yard, and the tracks between Worton and Chestertown became a rail trail.

While we waited to interview Mr. Callaway in the station's outer office, we noticed that sitting in a corner was a large, old black safe clearly marked "NYP&NRR." The staff member we were chatting with told us that the safe had never been opened by anyone at MDDE. Nor had it ever been moved, since it weighed about a ton. Neither he nor anyone else on staff had any idea how it got there or what it might contain, but it made a handy place to put the office coffeemaker. On our way out, we questioned MDDE's assistant general manager, who informed us, "We just tell everybody that it's full of gold bricks."

On a trip through Seaford, Delaware, in 2016, we went looking for the junction of MDDE and NS and a convenient place to spot trains. We easily found Norfolk Southern's tracks through the center of Seaford, parallel to Cedar Avenue. Seaford's main business thoroughfare, called High Street, had an overpass over the tracks, but no trains passed beneath us while we waited. Then, as we left Seaford heading west, we heard the loud blast of a diesel horn from MDDE locomotive no. 1203 hauling four boxcars and bearing down on us to cross Stein Highway on MDDE's Cambridge to Seaford line. I found my camera just in time.

A group of railfans called the North Dorchester Railroad Group had been trying to organize a regularly operating Eastern Shore Scenic Railroad on 6.4 miles of unused track between the towns of Hurlock and Preston. They began negotiations with the state in 2005, offering to improve the tracks and lease the passenger coaches owned by the Town of Hurlock. MDDE had no objections, but Maryland's Department of Transportation delayed the project during the years it took to conduct feasibility studies, both state and private. Finally, in 2015, the organizers reported that they were in lease negotiations with state officials. However, when we crossed the railroad tracks while driving through Preston in June 2016, they looked

An NYP&N artifact in the headquarters of the modern-day Maryland and Delaware Railroad. *Author's collection.*

A Maryland and Delaware freight train crossing Stein Highway outside Seaford, Delaware. *Author's collection.*

abandoned and so overgrown as to be hardly visible, indicating that little physical work had been accomplished, at least at that end of the proposed line. The latest MDDE news is the 2019 appointment of a new president, Cathrin S. Banks, and the resumption of freight service to Tyson Foods in Snow Hill, Maryland.

During the 1970s, the Commonwealth of Virginia was also taking steps to keep its trains running for those citizens and businesses that depended on this link with the outside world. In 1976, the commonwealth formed a public agency called the Accomack-Northampton Transportation District Commission (ANTDC) to see that trains kept moving through the lower Eastern Shore. The Virginia and Maryland Railroad Company (V&M) was formed to take control of the trackage and ferry service between Pocomoke City and Norfolk. An affiliated company began to acquire rolling stock and car floats, but in 1981, the ANTDC purchased the old NYP&N route outright, terminated the V&M contract and formed a new operating entity called the Eastern Shore Railroad (ESRR), which would operate on federal subsidies.

In 1985, a marine engineering and construction firm called Canonie Atlantic purchased the ESRR. Canonie Atlantic was based in Michigan, but the firm was then constructing a sewer pipeline off nearby Virginia Beach. For two years, it used the ESRR to move coal delivered by Norfolk Southern from southwest Virginia through the Little Creek terminal across the bay and up the Eastern Shore to a power plant in Maryland. The ESRR continued to haul grain and fertilizer for Eastern Shore farmers, as well as massive cargo for Bayshore Concrete Products headquartered in Cape Charles City.

By 1987, Canonie Atlantic was losing enough money on the ESRR to announce it would abandon the railroad if no one wanted to buy it. ANTDC regarded an operating railroad as a matter of public interest, even if it made no profit and sought financial help from the States of Maryland, Virginia and Delaware to buy ESRR back and keep it running. On February 12, 1987, the *Richmond Times Dispatch* announced that after weeks of negotiations, a sale agreement had been worked out during an all-night session in the offices of bank attorneys in Norfolk. All ESRR's stock, equipment and debt would return to ANTDC, and ESRR trains would continue to run on the old NYP&N route into the 1990s.

A car float docked at Cape Charles City in the 1970s. Freight operations continued with the Eastern Shore Railroad, formed in 1981. *Cape Charles Historical Society, Photograph by Ed Sharpe.*

During the 1990s, Eastern Shore residents began to question the operations of ESRR as a publicly owned railroad that collected state and federal subsidies but paid no local property or real estate taxes on its holdings, while making financial reports public only under pressure. In 1995 and 1996, ESRR president J.T. Holland responded that the railroad would submit to an outside audit. In 1996, ESRR got a new manager, Larry LeMond (later vice president of operations for the ESRR's successor, the Bay Coast Railroad). In a 1997 interview with the *Virginian Pilot*, published on March 9, LeMond admitted that the ESRR had been on a downhill ride, but it was making bond payments, had changed its barge towing contractor and was winning customers. LeMond expected that the forthcoming sale of Conrail to Norfolk Southern and CSX would bring the railroad more business.

The expected sale was completed in 1999, when Norfolk Southern acquired 58 percent of Conrail, including the Delmarva route between Newark, Delaware, and Pocomoke City, Maryland, which it named its "Delmarva Secondary." Norfolk Southern also acquired trackage rights over Amtrak's Northeast Corridor in Delaware and the "Newcastle Secondary" to the Port of Wilmington. In 2016, Norfolk Southern leased its Delmarva lines south of Porter, Delaware, to an operator called the Delmarva Central Railroad Company, a subsidiary of Carload Express.

The ESRR linked up with Norfolk Southern in Pocomoke City, and during the early years of the 2000s, the railroad continued to haul coal, grain, concrete products and other commodities. It also continued car float operations with leased tugboats.

While the railroad limped into the twenty-first century, so did the town of Cape Charles City. It did acquire a new industry in 1961 on the south side of the harbor, where Bayshore Concrete Products opened to manufacture concrete pilings for the Chesapeake Bay Bridge-Tunnel. The firm stayed on to manufacture other concrete products after the bridge-tunnel was built. In 1975, a Houston firm called Brown and Root purchased 1,900 acres of the old Scott family Hollywood Farm outside the town, with plans to fabricate offshore oil drilling rigs. It held on to the property when these plans were placed on hold.

Over a decade passed before Brown and Root executives met with Cape Charles City's town council and the county's board of supervisors in 1988 to unveil plans to develop the land into a community of single-family residences, townhouses and condos. After all, to the north were the thriving resorts of Rehoboth, Delaware; Ocean City, Maryland; and Chincoteague, Virginia. Just south, across the bridge-tunnel, was the resort area known as Virginia Beach. The area in between had remained a pristine Elysium, or a redneck wasteland, depending on one's point of view. Surely, many city and suburb dwellers from Norfolk, Baltimore and Washington, D.C., could be tempted to buy a shore retreat or a retirement home on the undeveloped lower Eastern Shore.

By that time, the town of Cape Charles City was pretty run-down. Its beach and boardwalk had washed away, its main street boasted few remaining businesses and its population grew only thanks to subsidized housing. In 1986 and 1987, the town had mounted a revitalization effort that included dredging the harbor, restoring the beach and renovating shop fronts in an attempt to attract tourists, but many locals had come to embrace the town's isolation and viewed any influx of outsiders as "people pollution."

Farther north on the Delmarva Peninsula in Parksley, the Eastern Shore Railway Museum was established in 1988. This tourist attraction celebrated the region's railroad heritage with an open-air museum housing a relocated NYP&N railroad station, a tool shed, a crossing guard shanty and quite a few restored railroad cars that visitors could tour with a guide. Most of the rolling stock on display had not run on the nearby NYP&N tracks, but visitors could see a dining car, Pullman car, parlor car, boxcar and a couple of cabooses from various American railroads. When we visited in 2014, our guide explained that some of this rolling stock had been donated, while other cars were simply parked there by private owners. She also explained that the museum's proximity to Chincoteague brought in many folks staying at that shore community who wanted a break from the beach or who had arrived too early to check into their hotels. Inside the building housing the site's museum and gift shop, we found many NYP&N artifacts and photographs.

South of Cape Charles City, Kiptopeke State Park was created in 1992 when a campground with a beach, boat ramp and fishing pier were installed roughly where the old ferry terminal building used to be. Finally, in 1996, Cape Charles City opened its own tourist attraction—a museum and welcome center in an old power generation station just outside of the town. The local historical society furnished the building with railroad artifacts dating to the 1880s, plus an excellent collection of photographs of NYP&N railroad and ferry operations over the years.

Meanwhile, Brown and Root kept waiting for the zoning changes that would allow them to begin construction of what they planned to call Accawmacke Plantation. By the mid-1990s, they had sold some of their undeveloped land for a sustainable technology industrial park where it was hoped that energy-efficient, non-polluting industries would establish

Opposite, top: The Eastern Shore Railway Museum has a beautifully restored dining car with original kitchen. *Author's collection.*

Opposite, bottom: At the Eastern Shore Railway Museum, you can see the compartments in a Pullman car. *Author's collection.*

Above: Rolling stock at the Eastern Shore Railway Museum. *Author's collection.*

themselves to create jobs for the community. The park waited five more years for its first tenant.

During the mid-1990s, Brown and Root also sold some of their land to a Virginia Beach firm called the Baymark Construction Corporation, headed by a man named Richard "Dickie" Foster. Foster planned to use it for what Brown and Root had wanted for years, namely a residential vacation and retirement community. Baymark had already constructed numerous developments south of the Norfolk–Virginia Beach expressway and throughout Virginia Beach.

Foster's plans for Hollywood Farm included three thousand housing units, two golf courses and a marina. He envisioned not a retirement community so much as a sophisticated active adult community. He was also quoted by local papers as being anxious to make Cape Charles City a "viable town." Despite naysayers' complaints about increased traffic,

The Cape Charles Museum and Welcome Center. *Author's collection.*

Railroad artifacts at the Cape Charles Museum and Welcome Center include rolling stock and a watchman's shelter. *Author's collection.*

housing density and strain on the sewer systems that had held up previous development plans for years, the community that Foster named Bay Creek began rising. Local property values increased, and the lower Eastern Shore got its first modern supermarket.

In 2004, Foster purchased what was left of the industrial park that had never taken off and put Cape Charles City back in the pages of the *New York Times*. In an article published September 3, 2004, titled "Waking Up Cape Charles," a reporter described the town's recent relative economic boom. It then had shops, restaurants and a hotel about to open. The reporter interviewed folks from Raleigh, North Carolina, who had recently purchased property, who mentioned that while one still could not buy feta cheese or a decent pair of shoes in town, they felt confident that "it will grow and change like every other area near the water, especially when people find out about this [Bay Creek] community."

When we visited in 2014, the Bay Creek community had two golf courses. Its Arnold Palmer course had been interwoven with a Jack Nicklaus course, and both were busy with golfers as we drove through Bay Creek on our way to its clubhouse, called the Coach House, for lunch. Besides its bar and casual dining restaurant, the Coach House housed a pro shop and served as the place where players picked up their carts. We had been told by folks we met in town that the mounds and bunkers of both golf courses had all been constructed on very flat ground from earth that had been trucked in. Bay Creek Parkway, which ran down the center of the community, was framed with lushly flowering foliage. Outside the Coach House door, we found embedded in the walkway a large millstone. A nearby plaque told us that this bit of architectural ornament had come from William L. Scott's house, where it had been intended to bring good luck to visitors who stepped on it. It was nice to see that Scott remembered where his farm had been so significantly transformed.

In 2005, Dickie Foster also got control of the railroad once operated by Scott and Cassatt when he signed a thirty-year contract with ANTDC to run the Eastern Shore Railroad, changing its name to the Bay Coast Railroad and saving it from the extinction planned by some local politicians who wanted to turn its northern segment into a bicycle trail. At the time, Canonie Atlantic was still involved and owned all the railroad's actual assets, but ANTDC owned all of Canonie Atlantic's shares. Once in control, Foster proceeded to invest cash in improved infrastructure, and by 2008, freight traffic was improving. The railroad continued to move grain, propane gas and materials for Bayshore Concrete Products.

In 2008, the Bay Coast Railroad reinstituted passenger service. The railroad purchased a diesel-powered restored 1913 interurban car (trolley car). It was fitted out as a parlor car for use on weekend excursions out of Cape Charles. The idea was to make it a party car, serving food and drinks on two-hour round trips. The car made its inaugural run in the spring of 2008 but failed to attract sufficient passengers, so the railroad put it up for sale in 2011. It left Cape Charles on a flatbed trailer in 2014 for use on another short line in Wisconsin.

The passenger party train might have been another victim of the housing downturn that began in 2008, stalling sales in Bay Creek's residential developments. Foster began selling land. Houses that had been constructed on speculation were offered at greatly reduced prices. Lawsuits were brought between Foster and another original Bay Creek developer named Paul Galloway. Another community under development north of Cape Charles proper was sold at foreclosure.

Slowly, the real estate market came back, and so did property values in the Bay Creek development. In 2012, a New Jersey entrepreneur purchased Foster's foreclosed development called Kings Bay and Marina Village, with plans to reopen a restaurant and shops on the site.

During the recovery period, the town of Cape Charles City expanded the harbor with new floating docks and arranged a deal to provide mariners with another amenity: a casual waterside bar and restaurant that could be a venue for local performers. The town began organizing festivals in its harbor area and repaired roads and sidewalks in the town.

Today, Cape Charles City makes for an interesting walking tour. The Cape Charles Historical Society provided us with a printed guide describing most of the town's architecturally and historically significant houses and buildings. The historical society also had many photographs of the town during the century and a quarter of its existence.

When we visited in 2014, we dined at that harborside restaurant called the Shanty, as well as the upscale restaurant then called Aqua in the Marina Village section north of the town. When we returned in 2016, Aqua had closed and reopened as a somewhat less upscale and more casual operation called the Oyster Farm Seafood Eatery, but the shops once intended for Marina Village had yet to materialize. Cape Charles City also had several cafes and gourmet markets offering takeout items, an Irish pub and an ice cream place. As of this writing in 2020, the town has many more dining options, both elegant and casual.

The resort communities north and south of the town proper were apparently designed as gated communities, but we had no problems getting access and driving around. The gate at the golf course communities south of the town was the only one actually staffed, but the guard let us through when we told him we wanted to have lunch at the Coach House. We could have rented a house in one of the resort communities, but both times we stayed at the Hotel Cape Charles on Mason Street. The proprietor told us that the building housing our hotel had always offered lodgings, but this particular iteration had opened in 2011. Both times, we chose a room with a balcony, from which we could look out over the old NYP&N rail yard across to the harbor. It would have been nice to see a Bay Coast train pull in, but we had no such luck on either visit, and staff members at the Cape Charles Museum and Welcome Center told us that very, very rarely did a train rumble by on the tracks behind their property.

I learned what I could about Bay Coast Railroad (BCR) before we drove down to Cape Charles in 2014. At that time, the railroad advertised itself as a short line that could handle traffic from the Northeast and Canada through its Norfolk Southern exchange at Pocomoke City. Its online material stated that it was "strategically located" between these northern connections and its western connections with Norfolk Southern and CSX on their terminal track around Little Creek, where the railroad classified traffic for these two carriers. The railroad's advertising also mentioned that the railroad could act as a bypass for the busy Northeast rail traffic corridor.

According to Bay Coast Railroad's advertising, its car floats traveled twenty-six miles across the Chesapeake Bay, pulled by contracted tugboats, a trip that took about twelve hours. The car floats had been officially out of commission for a while in 2009, when one of them was discovered to have structural problems, but the county's board of supervisors had secured state aid, so by the end of 2010, local news outlets reported that the car floats were once again running and anticipated to make a trip about once a week.

I had hoped to see a car float leave or arrive at Cape Charles, but when I interviewed Larry LeMond, vice president of Bay Coast's operations, in 2014, he quickly disabused me of that notion. He used the word "dinosaur" to describe the car float operation. The car floats required too much maintenance and had long been a money loser for the railroad. Mr. LeMond said he'd run a car float only if a customer could manage to fill the float, which rarely happened. In fact, when he needed to move a crew from one side of the bay to the other, he drove his employees across the bridge-tunnel.

I had found some news reports of car float operations on the Bay Coast Railroad, but they seemed to be special occasions that were few and far between. On May 6, 2012, the *Baltimore Sun* reported that a Bay Coast car

A rare sighting of a car float in operation in recent years. In 2012, the Bay Coast Railroad transported World War II gun barrels headed for a museum. *Cape Charles Historical Society, Photograph Collection.*

float had carried a sixteen-inch gun barrel used on the battleship *Missouri* during World War II, which was ultimately headed for a museum in Delaware's Cape Henlopen State Park. The navy had donated the gun, which was sixty-eight feet long and weighed 120 tons. Local groups had raised the cash for its transportation, and BCR had brought it across the Chesapeake to Cape Charles City, where it continued up the Delmarva by rail to Norfolk Southern and then via the Delaware Coast Line Railroad to Cape Henlopen.

In 2014, Mr. LeMond told us that Bay Coast then employed seven full-time and six part-time employees. Bay Coast trains moved chemicals, grain and products from the Bayshore Concrete Products, which had remained in operation. The railroad did more business on the Norfolk side of the bay, where it moved plastics, pipes and scrap steel. Most transfers with Norfolk Southern in Pocomoke City happened at night when Norfolk Southern opened the bridge over the Pocomoke River to make the connection.

When we finished talking with Larry LeMond and left the little trailer that housed the headquarters of the Bay Coast Railroad, Mr. LeMond said it was okay for us to walk around the rail yard and take pictures. We located the slip where the car floats once pulled in and walked right up to the transfer bridge that used to carry boxcars from land onto the car floats, noting its double tracks that switched into four tracks that would match the parking areas on the floats. If we had not known this railroad's history or what the car floats were meant to do, it might seem like the rail yard had tracks intended to lead cars into the drink. Across the harbor, we could see the concrete plant and hear the noises of its operations. The rail yard itself held two locomotives, one in Bay Coast blue livery and another painted black and still marked "Eastern Shore." There were several empty boxcars lined up on the tracks and two nice-looking parlor cars. Mr. LeMond had explained that one was privately owned and simply parked on the premises; the other, called the Southern Comfort, was sometimes used by visiting Norfolk Southern personnel as overnight lodging.

We saw several other people crossing the rail yard on foot, heading for the marina or the Shanty restaurant. The only other way to get there is

The bridge that freight cars rolled across to be positioned on car floats. *Author's collection.*

Rolling stock in the rail yard while it still belonged to Bay Coast Railroad. *Author's collection.*

One locomotive at the old Bay Coast rail yard still bore the Eastern Shore Railroad insignia. *Author's collection.*

over the Hump and down another road, not a readily walkable distance. No one seemed to spare a passing glance at the rail yard's features or the BCR rolling stock.

When we returned to Cape Charles City in 2016, I wandered through the rail yard again, that time in the evening and early morning hours, when I hoped that I would be able to trespass at leisure without encountering any inquisitive Bay Coast employees. This time, my investigations were guided by a framed map in the Cape Charles Museum and Welcome Center showing William L. Scott's estate circa 1887, with a diagram of the NYP&N terminus so that I could compare what I was seeing with what had once been located on the site.

The circa 1887 map showed me the tracks leading to the terminus splitting, with a line curving sharply southwest across a creek and a marshy area to the south side of the harbor, which was clearly marked "Scott's RR Siding." These tracks ran past a building marked "ice house" and several others marked "oyster p," presumably oyster packinghouses. Apparently, it was not just the produce of Hollywood Farm being shipped from this point.

Other incoming tracks split southwest toward the car float slip past a coaling place, where they could apparently be switched into a roundhouse. Still more incoming tracks continued due west to terminate at a building just north of the slip marked "station" and another north of the harbor marked "freight house." The station stood adjacent to what seemed to be a small garden echoing the design of the city's planned central park.

The staff at the Cape Charles Museum and Welcome Center also provided me with access to their extensive photo collection, so I saw images of the shops and power plant under construction around 1910. Sadly, there was no sign of these massive brick buildings with oversize windows and clerestories to let in the light. I had also seen images of the rail yard in its 1920s heyday, showing steam locomotives and rows of boxcars lined up on the multiple tracks of the enlarged rail yard, as well as loaded car floats pulled into the harbor's slip. I had seen the railroad's station and headquarters building just northeast of the slip and the very long freight house with the words "Cape Charles" emblazoned on its front façade and across its roof, presumably for the benefit of airplane passengers.

Standing on the Hump in 2016, I could still see the tracks leading into the rail yard, with the one line still leading southwest into what had been Mr. Scott's siding. The trailer that was then the headquarters of Bay Coast Railroad seemed to be more or less on the spot the railroad's old station and office had once occupied. The modern rolling stock seemed to be

A view of the rail yard just before the demise of the Bay Coast Railroad. The many vacant tracks hinted at the volume of former NYP&N business. *Author's collection.*

parked on tracks that once led to the freight house and ferry terminal. The landscaped area that had once separated the railroad property from Mason Street was in the process of being claimed by parking lots and commercial buildings.

One gentleman at the Museum and Welcome Center clued me in to where the modern railroad moored its remaining car float, which had not been visible to me from the slip, or as far out onto the transfer bridge as I had been willing to venture. From the public beach at the foot of Mason Street, I was able to work my way around the end of a chain link fence to a large area of largely vacant railroad real estate, where a big sign faced the harbor, warning boat owners not to dock their vessels there. Beneath my feet would have been the foundations of the freight house. I could see the concrete bulkhead that had replaced an earlier one. It still had intact the large cleats where ferry steamers would have been secured. Off in the distance, I spotted the long, low profile of the car float. Google Earth gave me a better image of what the car float looked like when it was docked at the transfer bridge on the slip.

A view of Bay Coast Railroad's little used car float operations from the vacant ferry dock. *Author's collection.*

I'm glad I got a chance to explore in 2016, because in May 2018, a local newspaper, the *Cape Charles Mirror*, reported that the Bay Coast Railroad was shutting down for good. The Delmarva Central Railroad had filed to lease and operate its upper fifteen miles between Pocomoke City and Hallwood, Virginia, where the railroad still had customers. A Virginia short line called the Buckingham Branch Railroad would be taking over BCR operations across the bay. The remaining BCR tracks would see trains operate no more. Local officials were considering turning the nearly fifty miles between Hallwood and Cape Charles into a rail trail.

In 2019, BCR's final owners were trying to sell the land occupied by the rail yard. Its ultimate repurposing had yet to be determined and would likely depend on zoning. When I stood on the site in 2016, I thought the old freight house location would make an excellent site for a resort hotel. It would have water views on three sides, though one of them would unfortunately face Bayshore Concrete Products across the harbor. By the spring of 2018, it seemed like that would no longer be a consideration. The *Virginian Pilot* reported that work at Bayshore would cease by the end of the calendar

A tribute to the NYP&N on the beach at Cape Charles City. *Author's collection.*

year. Bayshore had lost a bid to make precast concrete for the proposed construction of a new tube for the Chesapeake Bay Bridge-Tunnel. The ninety-acre plant was up for sale.

The decision to scrap the tracks, rolling stock and railroad buildings in the old yard presented a great opportunity for the Cape Charles Historical Society, albeit an expensive one. In the fall of 2018, BCR owners offered to donate much of this material to the society, providing the society moved it all to its own site. By early 2019, the society had transferred to its own sidings what it identified as a 1950s locomotive, a gondola car, a flat car and a tanker car, thanks to the sponsorship of a firm called Coastal Railway Construction Inc.

The society's most interesting acquisition was the pilot house of one of the old barges that had been put into operation in 1949. This barge, called the *Captain Edward Richardson/Nandua*, had sunk in the harbor in 1981 but had been salvaged and its pilot house moved to the rail yard, where it then served for many years as the railroad's headquarters building. In 2019, the society also moved this structure to its site, where it planned to use it as exhibition space, as well as an NYP&N artifact in its own right.

If the old rail yard ever does support a fine new resort, or even a Holiday Inn, it's comforting to know that the last relics of the NYP&N remained in Cape Charles City, the town that this railroad built. During the two opportunities that I had to wander the rail yard, it had seemed to me a lot like walking around the Acropolis, where the columns and caryatids paid homage to a way of life that was irretrievably gone. It's comforting to know that in Cape Charles City, one can still find and study the history of a transportation system that transformed an entire tri-state region and long stood as a testament to American ambition and know-how—the once celebrated New Line to Norfolk.

Bibliography

Primary Sources

Carl Zigrosser Collection. Numbers C-6 through C-11. Cassatt Family Papers. Philadelphia Museum of Art. Philadelphia, PA.

McComb Diary. Call Number 0699. Hagley Museum and Library. Wilmington, DE.

New York, Philadelphia & Norfolk Railroad Company Annual Reports. fHE 2791.N585 A2. Hagley Museum and Library. Wilmington, DE.

Pennsylvania Railroad Company. Accession Number 1807. Board Minutes. Hagley Museum and Library. Wilmington, DE.

Pennsylvania Railroad Company. Accession Number 1807. Lines East Predecessors and Subsidiaries. Hagley Museum and Library. Wilmington, DE. Materials for the following railroads:

Baltimore, Chesapeake & Atlantic Railroad Company
Baltimore and Eastern Shore Railroad
Eastern Shore Railroad Company
Maryland, Delaware and Virginia Railway
New York, Philadelphia & Norfolk Ferry Company
New York, Philadelphia & Norfolk Railroad Company
Norfolk and Portsmouth Belt Line Railroad
Peninsula Railroad Company (Maryland)
Peninsula Railroad Company (Virginia)

Philadelphia, Wilmington and Baltimore Railroad Company
Queen Anne's Railroad Company
Virginia Ferry Company

Uriah Hunt Painter Papers. Collection Number 1669. Painter Letterbooks, 1882–84. Historical Society of Pennsylvania. Philadelphia, PA.

Uriah Hunt Painter Papers. Collection Number 174. Chester County Historical Society. West Chester, PA.

William Augustus Patton Letters, 1899–1918. Collection Number Am.1116. Historical Society of Pennsylvania. Philadelphia, PA.

Secondary Sources

Allen, John L. "From Cabot to Cartier: The Early Exploration of Eastern North America, 1497–1543." *Annals of the Association of American Geographers* 82, no. 3 (September 1992): 500–21.

Arber, Edward, ed. *Travels and Works of Captain John Smith, Part I*. Edinburgh, Scotland: John Grant, 1910.

Barksdale, Francis. "A.J. Cassatt." *World's Work* 2 (July 1901): 972–77.

Breck, Samuel. *Sketch of the Internal Improvements Already Made in Pennsylvania*. Philadelphia, PA: M. Thomas, 1818.

Churella, Albert J. *The Pennsylvania Railroad*. Vol. 1, *Building an Empire, 1846–1917*. Philadelphia: University of Pennsylvania Press, 2013.

Clark, Charles B. *The Eastern Shore of Maryland and Virginia*. New York: Lewis Historical Publishing Co., 1950.

Cleveland, Frederick Albert, and Fred Wilbur Powell. *Railroad Finance*. New York: Appleton and Company, 1912.

———. *Railroad Promotion and Capitalization in the United States*. New York: Longmans, Green, and Co., 1909.

Daggett, Stuart. *Railroad Organization*. Cambridge, MA: Harvard University Press, 1924.

Davis, Patricia Talbot. *The End of the Line: Alexander Cassatt and the Pennsylvania Railroad*. New York: Neale Watson Academic Publications, 1978.

Dickon, Cris. *Images of Rail: Eastern Shore Railroad*. Charleston, SC: Arcadia Publishing, 2006.

Hayman, John C. *Rails Along the Chesapeake: A History of Railroading on the Delmarva Peninsula, 1827–1978*. Pittsburgh, PA: Marvadel Publishers, 1979.

Heinemann, Ronald L., John G. Kolp and Anthony S Parent. *Old Dominion, New Commonwealth: A History of Virginia 1607–2007*. Charlottesville: University of Virginia Press, 2007.

Hill, Robert White. *The Chesapeake Bay Bridge-Tunnel: The Eighth Wonder of the World*. New York: John Day Co., 1972.

Hudson, James F. *The Railways and the Republic*. New York: Harper & Brothers, 1886.

Kennedy, J.P. "A Legend of Maryland." *Atlantic Monthly* 4 (July 1860): 29–44, 141–52.

Lewis, Jim. *Cape Charles, a Railroad Town*. Eastville, VA: Hickory House, 2004.

Lockhead, John L. "The Boat Trains." *National Railway Bulletin* 43, no. 5 (1978): 18–19.

Mariner, Kirk. *Off 13: The Eastern Shore of Virginia Guidebook*. Onley, VA: Book Bin, Inc., 1987.

Matthew, J. Cecil. "Railroads of the Eastern Shore." *National Railway Historical Society Bulletin* 34, no. 1 (1969): 39–49.

Mayer, Brantz. "Old Maryland Manners." *Scribner's Monthly Magazine* 17 (January 1879): 315–31.

Moomaw, W. Hugh. *Virginia's Belt Line Railroad: The Norfolk & Portsmouth, 1898–1997*. Gloucester Point, VA: Hallmark Publishing Co., 1998.

Morrison, Samuel Eliot. *The European Discovery of America: The Northern Voyages, AD 500–1600*. New York: Oxford University Press, 1971.

Olmsted, Frederick Law. *A Journey in the Seaboard Slave States with Remarks on Their Economy.* New York: Dix and Edwards, 1856.

Parramore, Thomas C., Peter C. Stewart and Tommy L. Bogger. *Norfolk: The First Four Centuries*. Charlottesville: University Press of Virginia, 1994.

Pyle, Howard. "Chincoteague: The Island of Ponies." *Scribner's Monthly Magazine* 13 (April 1877): 737–45.

———. "A Peninsular Canaan." *Harper's New Monthly Magazine* 58 (May 1879): 801–17.

Rothrock, J.T. *Vacation Cruising in the Chesapeake and Delaware Bays*. Philadelphia, PA: J.B. Lippincott & Co., 1884.

Schotter, H.W. *The Growth and Development of the Pennsylvania Railroad Company*. Philadelphia, PA: Lane & Scott, 1927.

Steiner, Bernard C. "Traces of Claiborne's Settlement, Kent Island." *Johns Hopkins University Circular* 23, no. 165 (December 1903): 41–43.

Stover, John F. *American Railroads*. 2nd ed. Chicago: University of Chicago Press, 1997.

———. *The Railroads of the South, 1865–1900: A Study in Finance and Control.* Chapel Hill: University of North Carolina Press, 1955.

Whitelaw, Ralph T. *Virginia's Eastern Shore.* Richmond: Virginia Historical Society, 1951.

Wilson, Robert. "On the Eastern Shore." *Lippincott's Monthly Magazine* 18 (1876): 73–80, 233–43, 362–71, 467–76.

———. "Wye Island." *Lippincott's Monthly Magazine* 19 (1877): 468–74.

Wilson, W. Emerson, ed. *Mount Harmon Diaries of Sidney George Fisher 1837–1850.* Wilmington: Historical Society of Delaware, 1976.

Wilstach, Paul. *Tidewater Maryland.* Indianapolis, IN: Bobbs-Merrill Co., 1931.

———. *Tidewater Virginia.* Indianapolis, IN: Bobbs-Merill Co., 1929.

Wise, Jennings Cropper. *Ye Kingdome of Accawmacke on the Eastern Shore of Virginia in the Seventeenth Century.* Richmond, VA: Bell Book and Stationery Co., 1911.

Online Sources

America's Historical Newspapers. https://www.readex.com. Full content searchable text of many early American newspapers from 1690 to 1922. Available through subscribing libraries.

Eastern Shore Public Library and Virginia Center for Digital History. "Eastern Shore." Countryside Transformed: The Railroad and the Eastern Shore of Virginia, 1870–1935. http://eshore.iath.virginia.edu. This site has text extracted from local newspapers and maps and many images scanned from local repositories.

Hathi Trust Digital Library. https://www.hathitrust.org. *Railroad Gazette* and related publications *Railway Age* and *Railroad Age Gazette*, 1870–1907, are available in full text.

Library of Congress. "Chronicling America: Historical American Newspapers 1789–1922." https://chroniclingamerica.loc.gov.

New York Times on the Web 1851–Present. https://archive.nytimes.com. Full searchable text of back issues available through subscribing libraries.

Index

About the Author

Lorett Treese graduated from Bryn Mawr College and received a master's degree in American history from Villanova University's Graduate School of Arts and Sciences. For over twenty years, she was employed by Bryn Mawr College as college archivist. Before that, she worked as a systems analyst and programming manager. She has been writing books and articles about regional history for over thirty years. Her books include *The Storm Gathering: The Penn Family and the American Revolution*; *Valley Forge: Making and Remaking a National Symbol*; *A Serpent's Tale: Discovering America's Ancient Mound Builders*; and the first and second editions of *Railroads of Pennsylvania* and its companion volume, *Railroads of New Jersey*. Organized as travel guides, her previous railroad books covered the major railroads operating in the Middle Atlantic states. They explained the importance of railroads in the nineteenth and twentieth centuries and told the stories of individuals and events that shaped railroad history. She was a regular contributor to the magazine *Early American Life*, and her articles have also appeared in *Pennsylvania Heritage*, *Pennsylvania Folklife*, the *Magazine Antiques* and *Italian-Americana*.